everybody welcome

the course where everybody helps grow their church

Bob Jackson
and George Fisher

Leaders' Manual

CHURCH HOUSE
PUBLISHING

Church House Publishing
Church House
Great Smith Street
London SW1P 3AZ

ISBN 978 0 7151 4284 4

Published 2009 by Church House Publishing
Second Impression 2011

Designed and typeset in Ergo 10.5pt by Jordan Publishing Design,
Salisbury, Wiltshire
Printed in England by Halstan & Co. Ltd, Amersham, Bucks.

Contents

Introduction

Why welcome?

If most of the people who come into contact with your church actually join it, then you do not need this course. In fact you probably should have written it yourself!

But, if your church is more typical of churches in the developed world then under 10 per cent of the people who try you out will actually join. We know this from researching how many of the people who accept an invitation to 'Back to Church Sunday' become regular attenders, and from the 'Church Life Survey' in Australia. If you want to put that right, and encourage far more of the people who try out your church to end up belonging to it, this is the course you have been waiting for!

It is true that some people decide that church is not for them, or they pick a different church to join. But often the problem is the poverty of our welcome and, in particular, the difficulty of finding a route from attending a church service to belonging to its community. Increasing the percentage of people who 'stick' is the most promising and fruitful way we have of helping people transform their lives by joining the worshipping community and meeting God. It is also, therefore, the most fruitful way we have of growing our churches.

I (Bob) have been the visiting preacher at literally hundreds of churches. Even if my wife arrives with me, she tends to become invisible at the church door. All too often where I have been feted, my wife has been ignored from the moment she received a hymn book to the moment she finished her coffee. I should add that my wife really enjoys meeting people. But in most churches nobody even takes the trouble to say 'hello' and find out. Almost invariably, if church leaders have told me in the vestry what a friendly church this is, then my wife will assuredly have been ignored – what they mean is they are so friendly with each other they have no inclination to befriend the stranger.

Most churches think that they are friendly, but that is mainly because we are friendly with each other. We may say 'All are welcome' but not realize how unwelcoming we appear to the outsider.

Everybody Welcome is about removing the barbed wire, about making our welcome central to all we do and the

people we are. Just think what the impact would be if not 10 per cent but 25 per cent or even 50 per cent of the people who try out our churches succeed in becoming regular congregation members!

Some churches have been the subject of a 'mystery worshipper' exercise. A 'mystery worshipper' visits anonymously one Sunday and fills in a report form. Some churches get high scores in this exercise – people who are not normally churchgoers are pleasantly surprised by the contemporary accessibility of the worship and by the friendliness of the people. We should rejoice that there are many attractive, caring churches. But we should not get carried away by this. Our standards are much higher than those in the world around us and outsiders' expectations of church life are normally very low. But, most of all, friendliness on the day is only the start. True welcome is about active encouragement into the heart of the community of the church, and its job is not done until someone is completely at home, a valued, contributing member of the Body of Christ. Sometimes churches can appear superficially friendly to start with but fail to offer clear, enticing ways into the heart of the community.

Welcoming newcomers into the heart of the worshipping community is a ministry not just for the clergy or other leaders but for every member of every church. It only takes one to spoil a welcome.

One church had attracted a lot of new congregation members. A 'first-timer' wandered into the hall for coffee at the end of the service. An old hand, seeing them arrive, blurted out for all to hear, 'Not another bloody newcomer.' Another first-timer arrived rather well dressed at the village church. The sidesperson handing out the hymn books at the church door looked her up and down and said, as her opening remark, 'Oh, nobody wears a hat in this church.'

True welcome comes from the whole community, not just a couple of specialists. So work hard at encouraging the least-welcoming members of your church to attend as well as the naturals.

We've designed this course, therefore, for every church-going Christian who believes that belonging to their church is good for others as well as themselves. The title indicates not only that everybody should be made welcome but also that everybody should be welcoming. That is why the course will be most effective if you can persuade all or most of your church members to read the Members' Manual and attend Sessions 1–4.

The course is also relevant to every size of church. Small churches face different welcome challenges from large ones. For example, keeping an eye on people and getting contact details from them should be easier in a small church where newcomers are easier to spot. On the other hand, it may be harder in a small church to find that ideal someone who will be a natural first friend for the newcomer. So, if your church is particularly small or especially large, you may need to adapt the materials to suit. But the need for and the principles of welcome and integration are universal whatever the size of your church.

Everybody Welcome provides three routes for change:

1 It will help every individual in your church to have a welcoming approach to newcomers. This should happen simply through people participating in the course and does not require further formal action by the church. But it is important that as many church members as possible take part in the course.

2 It provides an opportunity to identify priorities for decision and change. At the end of the course the church council or other leadership group should identify priorities and then develop and implement an action plan for improving the church's welcome and integration of newcomers.

3 It creates a context for setting up a Welcome Team, whose specialist ministry is to take people from initial contact with the church through to becoming contributing members.

Welcome as a growth strategy

Before you commit to this course you may be wondering just how important is this 'Welcome' business anyway? I've been studying the factors involved in church growth for many years and I've reached a most surprising conclusion. At least it surprises me, and I'm sorry now that I've been so slow on the uptake.

We have focused on the rise of secularism, and of alternative spiritualities, the fast pace of contemporary life and the alternatives of contemporary living, the changing world in which the Church operates. They are all important. We have also focused on the ways that we in the Church organize ourselves, do evangelism and conduct ourselves in the world. These are just as important.

But the supply of people interested in being part of the Church has not dried up. Statistical enquiry shows that God is still giving us the people. A large-scale telephone survey sponsored by the Christian relief agency Tearfund suggested that three million people in this country would go to church if someone invited them. It's just that nobody ever has. Huge and increasing numbers of people are showing interest by attending church at Christmas. Most churches of any size have a constant trickle of people showing interest in them through the year. And most churches have a wide range of friendly contacts.

It is still Jesus' own job to draw all people to himself (Matthew 16.18) and he is still doing his job. The main problem and opportunity for the growth of the Church today is how well we who are already in the Church welcome the people whom God is sending us to join the Church. It is as surprisingly basic and simple as that.

For those of you who appreciate a mathematical approach, there is an appendix at the end of the book. This demonstrates using straightforward equations that, of all the alternative ways in which churches grow, increasing the retention rate of people trying us out is the most powerful. You can try putting your own church's statistics into the simple equations of the appendix and so follow through the impact of different strategies and approaches. You will almost inevitably find that sustained growth will not happen unless the retention rate is increased.

The need to focus on encouraging people to belong is partly because the rate at which that happens is currently so low that it weakens the power of other methods of encouraging people to find a home in the Body of Christ. I explain this more fully in the appendix. Working on welcome and integration, on the retention rate of those who try us out, is not an alternative to doing evangelistic missions. It is what has to be done to enable them to be successful again. Only a truly welcoming church can get the most out of an evangelist.

Welcome and the gospel

The hospitality of our welcome is central to our Christian calling. The gospel is about unconditional acceptance into the Body of Christ. Jesus said that he would be lifted up (crucified) so that 'everyone who believes in him may have eternal life' (John 3.15). Peter learned this lesson in Acts chapter 10 when, having accepted lodgings in the particularly smelly house of Simon the Tanner, he was taught in a vision to accept Gentiles as well as Jews into the church. Paul instructs us always to 'Practise hospitality' (Romans 12.13). The writer to the Hebrews urges us to 'Keep on loving each other as brothers. Do not forget to entertain strangers, for by doing so some people have entertained angels without knowing it' (Hebrews 13.2).

Welcome ministry is part of our response to God's ministry of reconciliation that he shares with his church.

> **All this is from God, who reconciled us to himself through Christ and gave us the ministry of reconciliation: that God was reconciling the world to himself in Christ, not counting men's sins against them. And he has committed to us the message of reconciliation.**
>
> *(2 Corinthians 5.18-19)*

There is huge power in effective welcome because it is the very expression of the gospel of reconciliation between God and humans, and between humans. The heart of the gospel is that all are called, all are included, all who ask to enter are allowed in to the kingdom of heaven.

> **You are all sons of God through faith in Christ Jesus ... There is neither Jew nor Greek, slave nor free, male nor female, for you are all one in Christ Jesus.**
>
> *(Galatians 3.26,28)*

In the world around we see alienation, isolation, division, barriers, people who are unwelcome here, there and almost everywhere. Who welcomes the refugee, the asylum seeker, the homeless, the ex-convict, the awkward eccentric, the apparent inadequate? Who seeks out the lonely widow hiding behind her fortress front door, or the depressive divorcee who has lost the confidence to make relationships? In the faithful Christian church it does not matter whether or not your face fits – we have a gospel of reconciliation, a core value of radical inclusivity, a community of welcome to all. There is no fee to pay to enter the Christian Church and you do not pay an annual subscription. You are not embraced because of what you can contribute. Your welcome, your inclusion, is based not on what you can give but on what can be given to you. You are welcomed in by grace, flowing from the supernatural love that God and his Church already have in their hearts for you.

If anyone did not deserve to be welcomed it was the prodigal son. He had betrayed his father, squandered his money and ruined his family's reputation. And yet, as the son skulked home in search of a servant's meal, the father, ever watchful, rushed out to embrace him while he was still a great way off. Such is the prodigious welcome of God the Father for all his children making the slightest gesture of return from afar to the warmth of his family home. And such should be the prodigious welcome of his Church to all who glance in our direction.

So we know the marvellous gospel theory that 'all are welcome' in the Church of Jesus Christ. Some churches would still seem to have older brothers too twisted to welcome the prodigal, gatekeepers who vet newcomers for suitability, snobs who give a warmer welcome to the respectable than the vulnerable, racists who check out skin colour. James (James 2.1-13) gives some straight teaching about the sin of favouritism when rich and poor come into our meetings. Jesus told us not to judge others or we too will be judged (Matthew 7.1). But other churches are genuine foretastes of heaven where all are welcomed, all are one, all are valued and all contribute to the whole.

So offering hospitality and welcome to all is not just a piece of tag-on good advice to churches. According to Jesus, how we respond to the stranger, to the neighbour in need, is determinative of our whole relationship with God. Look again at Matthew 25, at Jesus' teaching about the sheep and the goats given just before his arrest and trial. What is the distinguishing feature of the righteous sheep who receive their blessing and inheritance compared with the cursed goats who don't?

> **For I was hungry and you gave me something to eat, I was thirsty and you gave me something to drink, I was a stranger and you invited me in ...**
>
> *(Matthew 25.35)*

So Jesus says that when we welcome the stranger into the company of his Church we are actually welcoming him. When we don't welcome the stranger we are rejecting him, and are in danger of rejection ourselves. So hospitality, invitation, welcoming strangers into the family, goes to the heart of Christian community living. These are core values in the life of any church that wants to experience the blessing of God. The church that loves the people God is giving it to love, the church that welcomes God's strangers into the worship and community of God's people, will flourish, grow and hear the response of the King:

> **Come, you who are blessed by my Father; take your inheritance, the kingdom prepared for you since the creation of the world.**
>
> *(Matthew 25.34)*

So we know what we should be like even if we sometimes fall short of high standards. Often the reason we fall short is not our lack of willingness, our rebellion against the ministry of reconciliation, our resentment at the prodigals. It is our lack of confidence, our fear of straying out of our comfort zone, our awkwardness with the stranger, and preoccupation with our own needs or stress that breeds indifference to others.

Introduction

On our weaknesses God has compassion and yet he calls us to grow strong. This is where *Everybody Welcome* comes in – this course is designed to help every church that aspires to gospel standards of welcome and hospitality to put them into everyday practice. We can be the communities God intends us to be if we put our hearts and minds to the task, obeying and imitating the God of hospitality who welcomes every sinner to sit, eat and rejoice at his table.

Welcome and the big picture

The whole life, culture and strategy of the Church are bound up with its ministry of welcome and integration. It is central to how the local church fulfils Jesus' great commission – 'Go and make disciples of all nations' (Matthew 28.19). Making contact with people, befriending them, welcoming them into membership of the community of Christ and nurturing them into Christian discipleship can only be achieved when the quality of the life of the whole church measures up to the task in hand. This course is not about a small specialist ministry; it aims to bring new health and vitality to the whole of church life.

So it helps to see where every aspect of the course fits in to the overall picture. We are helping people through a life-changing, church-changing process of discovering the life of the church, then experiencing its worship, then belonging to its community, then contributing to its ministry. There are different aspects of each stage in the journey, and they are labelled and summarized in the chart below, which is our equivalent of a table of contents.

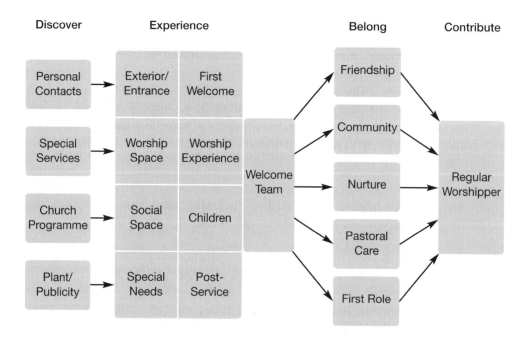

Overview: *Everybody Welcome* in five sessions

Session 1. Helping people discover the church's existence and character

People have to at least know about you, and may well need to know you in person, before thinking of becoming part of your group. So how does your church make contact with the local community and how can you become more visible in it?

Session 2. Giving people a good experience of the church premises

The church grounds, building and hall can attract or deter people. So how daunting is the physical business of entering your building for the first time? Can you develop your facilities to provide a positive and anxiety-free experience?

Session 3. Giving people a good experience of the church people

A newcomer's first experience of the church community usually determines whether they wish to join it. So how can your church offer a friendly, stress-free welcome to the local community? But people need to experience divine welcome as well as human. So how can you best give newcomers the chance to meet with God in your worship and other community events?

Session 4. Helping newcomers belong to the church community and start contributing to it

Church attendance should be a step along the way to Christian discipleship. Most people aspire to belong, not just to attend. The main factor in deciding whether someone stays is whether they make friends quickly. So how can your church be motivated, trained and organized to offer attractive friendship and belonging to newcomers? How can newcomers turn into members who exercise their own Christian ministry through the church?

Session 5. Integrating newcomers through the work of the Welcome Team

Some newcomers will be well picked up by individual enterprise. But probably many will not. A church that is serious about welcome has to designate and train a team of Welcomers with a clear and specific ministry of ensuring that new people become integrated into the community. So how can you best select, train and deploy your team so that every newcomer is offered a good welcome?

Introduction

Delivering the course

Course components

- comprehensive Leaders' Manual containing photocopiable checklists
- handy Members' Manual for use by all the course delegates
- Course DVD to accompany sessions 1–4.

For each session you will need

- photocopied checklists for each member
- pens for each member
- calculators for each small discussion group
- flip chart or overhead projector and screen
- video projector for DVD.

Formats

1   The course may work best if it runs for four evenings on successive weeks, or maybe they can be spaced out fortnightly or even monthly. Each session is timed to last 90 minutes and designed to take place in the church or church hall. Session 2 should certainly be in the church building itself. The fifth and final session is designed to provide focused training for those invited to be part of the church's Welcome Team.

2   Or all four sessions could be delivered at a single all-day conference one Saturday.

3   Or the course could be delivered through the cells or housegroup networks you have. If you go down this road you may wish to offer an extra group for people who do not normally belong to a regular small group. It is essential to collate the responses of all the small groups and perhaps to have a final get-together to compare notes. You will also need to make sure that each group has a DVD and a means of playing it, and that each group leader is equipped with a leaders' manual.

4   Each training session is designed to last for 90 minutes if everything runs smoothly and participants don't talk too much! If you are worried about over-running in your situation then you could advertise it to last 'up to one and three quarter hours'. Or you could cut a corner or two each time – we put some short-cut tips at the start of each session.

How the sessions work

The first four sessions are for the whole church. During this period, decide whom to invite to form a 'Welcome Team'. This team will have a special responsibility for helping people through from their first experience of the church to the point where they are a secure member making a significant contribution to it. So the final training session is for members of the Welcome Team only.

As you look through the Members' Manual you will see there are a number of suggested 'Over to you' exercises for members to do if they wish before each training session. Bear these in mind as you lead a training session – someone who tried one of the exercises might have something valuable to report.

There are a number of other possible 'Getting the feel of it' exercises suggested for each of Sessions 1–4 in this Leaders' Manual. There is no time for these within the 90-minute training session, but you could pick one and suggest that members try it out beforehand. Or you could advertise the start time of a training session half an hour early and begin with one or two 'Getting the feel of it' exercises. These help engage and prepare those of us who learn more from doing than thinking, from the flow of conversation than from the reading of books.

After an introduction each of the four main training sessions is divided into sections, each following the same format. For example, Session 1 'Discover' is divided into four sections that reflect the four main ways in which people discover the life and existence of a church – personal contacts, the church's programme, special services and its premises and publicity. Each section has some introductory material, usually on the DVD. Course members are then asked to respond by filling in a personal tick-box checklist and then talking through one or two discussion questions in pairs or small groups. Finally, at the end of each section or at the end of the whole session there is time for the small groups to report their main findings to the group as a whole.

The pre-reading is designed to inform and inspire course leaders. You can use sections as an informal script for what you want to say during the sessions or you can use it as a focus for your thoughts as you prepare for sessions.

Using the checklists

The personal checklists can be filled in quickly out of instinct or else thought about a bit more carefully. The personal checklist is the main tool for helping the church leadership to determine priorities for action to improve welcome at the end of the course.

If you find someone in your group unable to do the checklists because of a disability (e.g. visual impairment), encourage them to pair with someone else and to do it together.

At the end of the time allocated for filling in the checklists, comparing notes and discussing the questions at the end, the checklists should be handed in to someone with a calculator who should quickly work out the average score and announce it to the whole group.

It can be very useful for members to compare notes and work out why their scores – and therefore their perceptions of the church – differed from each other.

At the end of every session you will know the average score for each section. This will reveal where you think your strengths and weaknesses lie. At the end of the whole course it should therefore be possible for the church leadership team to work out priorities for change. How can the strengths be reinforced and the weaknesses tackled? Perhaps the aspects with the lowest score should be the top priorities for attention.

Introduction

Using the Members' Manual

The Members' Manual contains a slimmed-down version of this Introduction plus preparation reading for each of the four main training sessions.

Every participant should be given a copy of the course Members' Manual a week or two before the first session. During the week before each session they should be asked to read through the relevant part of the manual and spend some time praying and thinking about the theme and its implications for themselves personally and for your church corporately. It is particularly important that everyone prays about this, because it is your dialogue with God in prayer that will motivate and generate real change.

A note about Session 5 and the Welcome Team

It is a key assumption of the course that a church going through it will either already have a Welcome Team or be willing to consider setting one up.

From an early stage start thinking through the issue of the Welcome Team and Session 5. Read through the notes on Session 5 before the course begins and start planning the remit of your team and who to invite on to it.

Advance preparation

As with all things to do with the Christian life and church, our human efforts will be useless without prayer and without the work and power of the Holy Spirit. We believe that God the Holy Spirit has already been directing the church towards improving its welcome and hospitality – we can see this through the huge progress made by the 'Back to Church Sunday' initiative, which designates the last Sunday in September as a day for church members to invite friends, family and neighbours to come to church with them. This is backed up by publicity in the media. We can also see it through our research into how churches are growing and shrinking and in the reactions to the drafts and trials of this course. We are catching God's agenda for the church here. But, even so, heartfelt prayers are also needed to ensure that learning to love our new neighbours in the church is to bear fruit in the flourishing of Christ's Church and kingdom. So do please make praying for the success and impact of this course a priority for your church in the weeks leading up to its start! You may wish to include the Course Prayer in the prayer time in church services.

Further preparation tips

1   Advertise the event two to four months in advance and encourage every congregation member to sign up to attend, clearly stating the dates and venue. You can download a template of a poster from the web site into which you can insert your church's details. You might like to send a personal letter or invitation to every member and also to make an open invitation in church services. Use a list at the back of church, or emails, or a small group phoning around. Plan the dates of the course carefully to ensure maximum attendance and do not have competing events.

2 Ask as many people as possible to take on roles for the event, especially those whom you particularly want to be there. For example, you will need people to be responsible for the checklists, and also people to run the projector and DVD. Older children or teenagers could enjoy these jobs. You will also need people to do refreshments, welcome on the door, set up the room and tidy away at the end, read a Bible passage and so on. If you elect to deliver the course using small groups then lots of people will be involved anyway.

3 Decide whether the church will be buying the Members' Manuals (£3.99 each) or whether you are asking the members to buy them. Whichever way, buy them well in advance and make them available to pick up at church. Ensure there is a name on each of them so you know who has not got their manual yet. Everybody should have their manual at least a week before Session 1.

4 Do invite the whole church to Sessions 1–4. Not everyone will come, but try and get as many as possible. Pray hardest for and work hardest on the people who need the course the most! They may not make the most willing volunteers. However, only the people who have been asked to form the church's Welcome Team should be invited to Session 5. It is unlikely you will attract everyone to the course, but set yourself an ambitious target as the more people who attend the more effective the course will be – it only takes one person to spoil a welcome.

5 Make sure there are good sermons on the theme of welcome prior to the course beginning. There is plenty of material to help here in the Introduction to this book. This should help people catch the vision and sign up to attend.

6 If you are planning four evenings or a day event the venue will need to be large enough for the whole group to sit in comfortably and you will need to equip it with a data projector and large screen so that you can play the DVD clips. So it is likely to be your church hall or church, or perhaps a nearby venue that people enjoy going to.

7 Arrange the seating so that everyone can see the screen but can also talk in groups of two, three or four when comparing notes on the checklists.

8 Each Session is timed to last 90 minutes, but the leading of it will need to be slick in order to achieve this. We suggest those leading the event get together beforehand to check through exactly how it is going to be led and presented to keep it flowing.

9 Clearly, the aim of the course is to encourage your church to improve its welcome. In the end, the course will be a success if you are able to make a difference to the welcome offered week by week, not if you finish each session precisely according to the timings we've suggested here! Do aim to cover as much of the material as you can, but a session exceeding two hours will be off-putting.

10 We suggest you advertise the doors being open 30 minutes before the start of the session time and offer people a drink and a biscuit as they arrive. As they chat, encourage people to discuss their response to what they have read in the Members' Manual. Stop serving a few minutes before start time so that you can make a prompt start.

Introduction

11 In many ways it is easier and may be more natural to use the course with existing small groups. But remember this will be more expensive as each group leader will need a Leaders' Manual and each group will need its own DVD (or at least the Tuesday group will need to share one with the Thursday group).

12 Someone will need to copy and collate the photocopiable checklists included in the Leaders' Manual. For each session have enough sets (probably stapled together) for every individual who has signed up to come and have a few spares. It is very important to collect the checklists in efficiently and then to compile the scores together to report back at the end of the evening. The compilers will need a spare copy of each checklist to do the marking on and a calculator to work out the average score.

13 We recommend that you ask one or two people, who do not normally attend, to come to a service at your church a few weeks before you start the course. Details of how to do this are available on the web site **www.everybodywelcome.org.uk** The mystery worshippers should make their report during Session 3.

Before, during and after your own training events you can check out our web site **www.everybodywelcome.org.uk** where you will find further information.

Discover

Making the church more visible

■ Contents ■

■ Session 1 aim ■

The aim of this training session is to review the whole way the church contacts its community. It should help members – by which we mean regular attenders, whether or not they are on the electoral roll or other members' list – to see the role and purpose of the different aspects of church life more clearly, and to work out how their church can make itself more visible and attractive to outsiders. The session should help each member of the congregation review and enhance their own part in the church's ministry of reaching out to the wider community.

There are motives for reaching out to the wider community other than that of providing pathways for people to join the church – we all share the same kingdom imperative to love our neighbours in need however they respond. But we should also have confidence in the power of the gospel and the love of the Church to attract at least some of our contacts to journey on into the community of Jesus Christ.

■ Session 1 outline ■

Welcome Housekeeping notices and prayer .... 3 minutes

DVD Introduction and **The word on the streets** .... 4 minutes

Word on welcome Reading: Acts 2.42-47 with brief comment .... 6 minutes

Do we know anyone? Asking course members how many people they
know who might respond to an invite to a church event or service .... 2 minutes

Personal contacts checklist Individuals tick boxes, discuss in pairs
or groups then hand checklists in .... 11 minutes

What goes on at our church? Compiling a list of the elements of the
church's programme .... 6 minutes

DVD A church at the heart of its community
St Edmund's Whalley Range, Manchester .... 7 minutes

The church programme checklist Individuals tick boxes, discuss in
pairs or groups then hand checklists in .... 9 minutes

What special services do we have each year? Compiling a list .... 6 minutes

The special services checklist Individuals tick boxes, discuss in pairs
or groups then hand checklists in .... 9 minutes

DVD How do they do that? A church that raised its profile
Hope City Church Sheffield .... 6 minutes

The premises and publicity checklist Individuals tick boxes, discuss in
pairs or groups then hand checklists in .... 9 minutes

So what did we learn? Sharing ideas and conclusions, announcing
checklist results .... 10 minutes

DVD Authors' conclusion The two engines of change .... 1 minute

Course Prayer .... 1 minute

■ Session 1 leaders' notes ■

Welcome This is a course *about* welcome so make sure that everyone is well welcomed to the course! Have people on the door (ask the usual Sunday welcomers to do this?) and give a warm welcome from the front to start the event. Make sure that everyone has a pen – have some spares to hand out. Pray briefly – you may wish to use the Course Prayer printed out in the Members' Manual so everyone can join in.

> **Course Prayer**
>
> Heavenly Father, you have welcomed us into your kingdom
> and your heart's desire is to draw every human being to yourself.
> Grant us clear eyes to see people as you see them,
> sensitive feet to stand in their shoes,
> and warm smiles to welcome them in your name.
> Give us such generous hearts,
> that our church becomes a foretaste of heaven
> where every soul you send us finds their loving home
> in the community of your Son our Saviour Jesus Christ,
> Amen.

DVD Introduction and **The word on the streets** Have this ready to play as soon as the prayers are over. Try not to waste time and make people nervous with gaps between items. This clip only lasts five minutes, so have your reader ready to read as soon as it finishes. The aim of showing these interviews with passers by on the street is to help us see ourselves as others see us.

Word on welcome Have someone read Acts 2.42-7 and then make a very brief comment on it. This is not an excuse for a sermon! The comment should be along these lines:

The first church lived out its life pretty publicly. They were faithful to the teaching of the apostles and to the rhythm of prayer and breaking bread together. Awesome signs and wonders were performed. Their lifestyles were transformed as they gave up their personal wealth, and met outdoors in the city centre where passers-by could see them being full of joy praising God. In short, they got noticed, outsiders discovered what this new faith was about and they liked what they saw. As a result the Lord was able to add daily to their number those who were being saved. How do we in our church get ourselves noticed so that the Lord can add daily to our number?

Do we know anyone? Without embarrassing any individuals find out in general how many people were identified who may just accept an invitation to come to a church service or event (see the exercise in Session 1 of the Members' Manual). We suggest you ask, 'Hands up those who put ten or more, five to nine, two to five, one, zero.' Draw a simple conclusion – perhaps it is that we know lots of people who might accept an invitation (in which case let's ask them) or we know very few (in which case we need to concentrate on building up our friendships and contacts).

Personal contacts checklist Explain you are assuming that everyone has read the introductory input to each checklist. Invite them to fill in the personal contacts checklist pretty quickly, relying on feeling and instinct more than lengthy analysis. This should normally take three or four minutes but it may take longer for this the first of the checklists while members get the idea. Then ask them to compare notes in pairs or threes or fours. Did they score aspects in the same way as each other? Then, if there is time, they could discuss the questions at the end of the checklist, though it is likely that not every pair or group will get this far. At the end of the nine minutes allowed for this section get the checklists handed in. The people collecting the checklists should have a table in a corner of the room at which they can add up and average the results in the next few minutes. Make sure they are still in the same room and so can take in at least something of what follows.

What goes on at our church? Ask people to shout out the elements of your church's programme – its events, meetings, groups etc. Someone might list them on a flip chart or an overhead projector or with some fancy electronic gizmo through the data projector your elderly author does not understand.

Ask for a guess at the number of people involved in each who do not normally come to church. What does this exercise tell you about the power of your programme to introduce people to the life of your church?

DVD A church at the heart of its community The aim of this clip is to inspire people with the story of a church that has developed a programme that puts it at the heart of its community.

The church programme checklist Repeat the checklist exercise using checklist 2. Hopefully the compilers will have finished averaging the first checklist during the brainstorm session and can join in by filling in their own checklist before collecting up again.

What special services do we have each year? Find out if anyone has drawn significant conclusions from the 'Over to you ...' exercise in the Members' Manual. Ask people to shout out examples of the special services your church normally has during the course of a year. Someone might list them using the aforementioned flip chart, overhead projector or gizmo. Ask for a guess at the number of visitors or newcomers or fringe folk that each special service attracts. Which ones really work and which do not?

The special services checklist Repeat the checklist exercise using checklist 3.

DVD How do they do that? The aim of this clip is to show how one church has raised its profile.

The premises and publicity checklist Repeat the checklist exercise using checklist 4.

The compilers at this point should have already handed in the results of the first three checklists to the course leader. Their aim now is to have compiled the results of this checklist so they can be announced before the end of the meeting. If this is not possible, don't panic. The course leader will announce in a calm voice, as though this had always been the plan, that the results will be announced at the start of Session 2 of the course.

So what did we learn? In a large group the leader might invite each pair or small group to write down the main things they have learnt about the church's strengths and weaknesses and about the priorities for improving things. In a smaller group the leader may wish to take comments from the floor. Or the time could be divided between the two approaches. It is important that someone takes a note of the main things that are said so that they can be fed back to the church leadership for action. A compilation or summary could be handed out to everyone at the start of Session 2. Some changes do not require deliberation, decisions, budgets and so on. They can be made simply and quickly. So invite members to come up with one offer or change that they or someone else could implement straight away without it costing any money or being controversial. For example a youth leader might decide to set up a group text system with the youth group and their friends for invitations to and reminders about future events. Or someone might offer to be the church's link person with the art group that uses the premises on a Wednesday afternoon. She will organize a display of paintings with a harvest theme in the church next September and invite the group to the harvest service.

DVD Authors' conclusion – play this followed by the **Course Prayer**.

Time-saving tips In Session 1 you could prepare lists of the church's programme and of the special services beforehand. Hand them out at the appropriate time and simply ask if you have forgotten something or what strikes people about the lists. Each of these items is timed at six minutes, and tackling them this way should reduce the time needed considerably. Also, although filling in the first checklist might take a good nine minutes, by the last one people will have got the idea and may well be able to do it in five if encouraged to get a move on.

Session 1: Discover

Session 1 pre-reading

When you lead the session you will need to assume that people have indeed done their reading and exercises as there is no time in a packed programme to play catch-up. We all know that there will be some real people in most real churches who don't manage to read the introductions but they should still be able more or less to cotton on to what is happening! The Members' Manual includes a summary of, or excerpts from, the material below. Read through the longer material given here but also check what parts of it appear in the Members' Manual.

Discovery as the starting point

People will not join a church until they discover it. In order to have a chance of welcoming people to worship with us we first have to show them that a living and active church exists. It's surprising what people assume just from the look of the church building. I (Bob) had a wake-up call about the importance of the appearance of the church exterior years ago when three of the stained-glass windows at my church were smashed by vandals and got boarded up; some neighbours assumed that the church had closed down. After all, the door was always locked and barred when they were about, and now the glass was boarded up, making the building looking ready for demolition.

As well as the visibility of the church building, people discover a church through the activity of the church members. Churches need to live their lives visibly out in the open where others can discover their existence and begin to relate to them. We cannot welcome until we first make contact. Some churches have a low profile, very limited contact with their local community and, as a result, very few visitors. Others have a high profile, masses of contacts, a large fringe, and many people trying them out. So let's review the ways in which your church makes contact with people and how good you are at it. By and large there are four ways in which churches make contact with their local communities.

In Session 1 we look in turn at each of these ways of becoming visible. At the end of each of the four sections you will be asked to score a checklist. This will reveal where you think the strengths and weaknesses of your church lie. When your checklists are compiled with others they will reveal priorities for improvement.

As well as an agenda for the church council or leadership to pursue, this exercise should help you think through your own part in making the church more visible and attractive to the local community. The four main ways of becoming visible are:

1 Personal contacts

2 The church programme

3 Special events and services

4 Church premises and publicity

1 Personal contacts

This is so obvious it is easy to overlook. So take a moment to think about how many family, friends, acquaintances, neighbours and colleagues you know who do not go to church. Some Christians have got so immersed in church over the years that they know hardly any people who are not already Christians. How ironic that faithful commitment to God's church can suck Christians out of the very places where we are needed! It is also a disaster! Christians should not live in isolated ghettos but be salt in society, learning from and contributing to a wide range of other people.

If your church has so taken over your life that there is little else in it, you may like to consider how to start making friends with non-churchgoers again.

Over to you ...

Use your instinct to draw up a shortlist of people you know that may just accept an invitation to come to a church service or event. For some of you the list may be very short indeed but make it anyway! Write down the number of people you have identified in the box below and bring it with you to Training Session 1.

The number of people I can think of is:

The Tearfund survey mentioned in the Introduction found out how many people in Britain say they would like to go (often return) to church if only they were invited. The answer was three million! That's almost as many who go already. On average, each churchgoer will know at least one other person who does not have the courage to go to church alone but is hoping to be asked by someone who already does go. But so far they haven't been asked. So one or two of the people you have thought of might actually be thrilled to be invited!

So the first and most important way of making a first contact is personal and involves every church member. People discover our churches through us inviting them in.

Sometimes the first invitation will be to a social event or to some other element of the church's programme that is not an act of worship. Sometimes it is best simply to invite someone to a church service. This is what people expect us to be about, this is the heart of what we do and the best way to meet the church as a whole.

The great success of 'Back to Church Sunday' proves the importance of personal invitation. Invitation cards are given to church members with which to invite their

Session 1: Discover

contacts to church on the special day. In 2007 in the Diocese of Lichfield alone around 6,000 people accepted a personal invitation from churchgoers and went to church with them. Six months later a repeat survey found that between 700 and 900 of the 6,000 were now regular churchgoers. A further 3,000 still retained a contact with the church and had probably been back at least once, perhaps at Christmas.

So whom should you invite to church with you one Sunday, perhaps as part of your church's next 'Back to Church Sunday'?

There are many ways other than personal friendship through which people come into contact with churches. But even if the initial contact is through attending a church hall user group, or turning up at a carol service, or meeting the vicar through a funeral service, the key to the next step of turning up at regular worship events is probably personal invitation. So have a think about your own track record of invitation and about the general culture of your church.

There is more to this invitation business than merely deciding whom to invite and having the courage to do so. Pray for guidance not only about whom to invite but also when to invite them and to what event. And what else should the invitation include? In one church on 'Back to Church Sunday' the congregation decided to invite people not only to church on Sunday morning but also back to their own homes for Sunday lunch. Forty-five people accepted the invitations – after all it's quite rude to refuse an invitation to a meal in your friend's home! And remember that invitations are far more likely to be accepted when they come as a natural part of a growing relationship than as an awkward bolt from the blue.

For most people, a single invitation is not enough. Even if they come with you once it does not mean that they will now feel able to come under their own steam thereafter. Be sensitive and don't put someone off by overdoing things, but be prepared to invite people two or three or four or more times to services and events before they begin to feel sufficiently at home not to need further help.

2 The church programme

Churches offer all sorts of meetings, groups, events and services to their local communities. Collectively these can be called the church's 'programme' – the list of things the church does. Of course this list is often not the result of a fully thought-out strategy resulting in a coherent 'programme'. In many churches the list of what is done is more the piecemeal result of history. But let us call it the church's programme anyway!

Very often the programme is focused on community use of the church hall premises. Many churches have pre-school groups, pensioners' clubs, lunch clubs, youth clubs, open house cafes, or uniformed organizations meeting on their own premises. Many of these will attract members who do not attend regular church services.

There are two main routes into the worshipping community available for such people. One route is that the group they attend becomes a halfway house into church worship. A lady attends a lunch club and sits next to another lady who is a church member. They become friendly and she gets invited along one Sunday. Or else she is given an invitation card to a carol service, and, when she gets there, she is pleased to meet up with a couple of other lunch club members.

The other route is that the church takes steps to turn the event on the programme into 'church' for the people who attend it. For example, one church moved its weekday service to half an hour before the start of the lunch club. Most of the members started turning up half an hour early so that church worship, lunch and fellowship became part of the same event and experience. Another church held a regular Saturday morning men's breakfast with a speaker, some prayer and singing. Some of the men thought they were coming to a social event with a good cooked breakfast. But if it quacks like a duck and waddles like a duck, it's a duck. They had been to church.

One church started children's activities after school in shop premises on a deprived estate. After a while, these included some Christian teaching. After a few years on two evenings a week, the event started to include worship and prayer as well as Bible Study. Parents started coming along. A new church was born – growing out of, and being an integral part of, an existing ministry on the programme of the church.

Some churches turn their premises into a base for community action, perhaps calling it a 'social action centre'. The aim is simply to serve the local community but one outcome is usually that a lot more contacts are made. Many people are able to discover the life and people of the church through its community enterprise. Those who discover the love of God through the love of his Church may well end up as church members. A frequent experience is that non-church member volunteers and staff are more likely to find their way into the church community than are those the project is most designed to help.

Many churches will also hire out their premises to all manner of community groups for events that are not part of the church's own programme but still take place on church premises. These at least get people used to coming to the church premises and they open up new contact and discovery opportunities. Churches where the worship space is multi-purpose and available to let during the week have a particular advantage here – the premises ice has been broken.

Some churches simply see these user groups as revenue sources. Some even make the mistake of taking so many bookings (in order to balance the books) that the church can't use its hall for its own events. Other churches see the user groups as contact points and take steps to get to know them. One church appoints a link person for every user group. Their job is to attend the group regularly, ensure smooth relationships between the group and the church, and to befriend the members and introduce them to the wider life of the church.

In some churches the programme of community service will involve activities not based on the church premises at all. Examples include home visiting of the disabled and elderly people, gardening services to pensioners, debt advice, or charity fund-raising. One church has a large number of such 'touching points'. Three times a year it invites the contacts made to join an Alpha Course. Many people over the years have followed this route into faith starting with a touching point, then Alpha, then joining the worshipping community.

Session 1: Discover

Some churches have an annual round of fund-raising social events that involve a lot of others in the local community – the Christmas Fayre, the Summer Fete etc. These can be good fun, draw the church together, and be great points of contact with others. The danger is that the church is seen as an organization that is mainly interested in other people's money to keep them going. But there is also a great opportunity to develop links, to get noticed and to enable people to take the next step. At such events there should always be an invitation to a future special church service or event.

Hope City Church, Sheffield

Many churches have too big a programme. It is too big a burden and nothing is done very well. It is exhausting the members trying to keep things going and they are getting de-motivated. Often this situation arises as a legacy from the past and a fear of upsetting people or letting them down by closing ministries and activities down. Courage and vision are needed to slim down or re-jig the programme so that it is manageable to do it well and it is relevant to today's needs. A healthy church does a few things well. It concentrates on those that are the most effective today in forwarding the whole mission of the church: pastoral, evangelistic and social. From the point of view of hospitality and welcome of newcomers it concentrates on those that open up the best opportunities for people to get to know the church and the most natural opportunities for them to start joining it and meeting God.

> **Over to you ...**
>
> **Which groups and activities in your church have brought new people into the worshipping community over the last few years? Where do you think there is potential in the future?**

3 Special services and events

Some people discover our church through attending a special service or event. They may come along to the school harvest service their child is singing in, or the parade service with their son in 'Cubs', or to the crib service or Christingle or Midnight Communion Service the church puts on over Christmas. Or maybe they come to the 'Christian' pantomime or a Mission Weekend event. Others may attend a 'memorial service' the church holds once in a while for bereaved relatives from the funeral services the clergy have taken. For others it will be a wedding or a baptism or the funeral service itself. Some churches have a lot of 'civic'-type services and events perhaps for mayor-making or Remembrance Day.

Over to you ...

There are three main questions to ask yourself about your church's special services. First, do you have an appropriate range of them? Second, do people who are not already church members actually come to them? Third, how clear and how well travelled is the route from attending a special service to becoming part of the regular congregation?

Try listing the special services your church has over the course of a year to which non-members regularly come. Then make a guess at how many people attend them in total. You might be quite surprised by the number. So, is your church one with a lot of special services and so a lot of contact with people, or one with few of these opportunities?

Creating such opportunities may be part of your strategy for meeting new people and welcoming them into the regular worshipping community. But how well done are your events and do they act as any sort of way in to the rest of church life? One key issue is whether church members are also present at these events and whether they are on the lookout to talk to and welcome in people who may be interested. Memorial services have grown in popularity in recent years but they rarely result in people joining the regular congregation, usually because they are held at a different time and the regular congregation don't come.

So there is a strong case for having as many special services or events as possible at the normal service times so as to open up the route for those who attend the special service into the regular life of the church. If the special service is at its own time then it is important to have church members – especially the Welcome Team – present at it to make the connections for the visitors.

4 Church premises and publicity

What do your church grounds and buildings look like to outsiders? Do they have to hack their way through an overgrown graveyard to even glimpse the prison-like church door? Was it their Nan's funeral last time they came? If the buildings and grounds look unfriendly and are associated with negative feelings some people in your community will avoid them at all costs. Far too many of our buildings say to the passer-by either 'Closed' or 'Keep out'.

Over to you …

One evening this week wander round your church grounds and buildings trying to see them with a stranger's eye. If possible bring along a friend or neighbour who does not attend church and ask them to tell you the images and feelings conjured up inside them. What could be done to improve things?

Other church buildings are a great asset to our welcome – they look beautiful and well cared for, places for meeting with God. If you are able to keep the church unlocked during the day then do everything you can to encourage people to come in to find some quiet space, to pray, or just to enjoy the building. Offer refreshments if you can.

Other people discover the church's premises by attending an event or group in the church hall. What does the state of the hall say about the church as a community? Is it well cared for and good quality or a bit of a mess? If money is an issue it is often possible to find grants and outside finance to improve a church hall that has wide community use.

And what about your notice board? We'll ask your views in Session 2, but before then try looking at your notice board with an outsider's eye, or else bring a friend to look at it. Does it convey the right information in language people will understand? What unspoken messages about the church does its style and condition convey?

Most people today if they are looking for a church will browse the web. Will they find your church if they do so? At the very least every church should be on the 'A Church Near You' web site, and every church should consider having a web site of its own. This needs updating regularly and a webmaster is needed to keep it up to date and attractive.

I went to a fresh expressions-style church recently. A few months earlier we had appointed a young clergyman to plant a new church from scratch among younger adults whose lives revolve around relationship networks rather than geographical locations. The evening began with a barbecue on the steps of the building, followed by an act of worship inside. I chatted over burnt sausages to one young man, who said it was his first time. 'How did you hear about it?' I asked. 'On Facebook', he replied.

So keep ahead of the game – what new communications tools could effectively publicize your church? The early Church spread through using the cutting-edge communications technology of the day – the Roman road. What is the appropriate technology today for your church?

St Edmund's Whalley Range, Manchester

Ideas and links for web sites and other publicity and communications tools are available on our web site: **www.everybodywelcome.org.uk**

Electronic tools have not, however, entirely replaced the parish magazine. If you have a church magazine, who is it for? The most effective are those that are aimed at the whole local community. Let them be Christian in content and let them advertise the church's services and programme, but let them also be a useful tool for general community cohesion. If you can finance the magazine in some way, perhaps through adverts, and post it free through every letter box then so much the better. Look out, too, for ideas for parish magazines on the Church of England web site at **http://www.cofe.anglican.org/about/diocesesparishes/parishmags/**

But there is one way in which the magazine can be a turn-off today. If prominently displayed is a long list of church office-holders and job vacancies then it gives the church the image of being an organization with servants trapped into onerous voluntary jobs. Postmoderns will run a mile (or should that be 1.6 kilometres?) because they do not take well to being trapped by repetitive weekly commitments. It may be more effective to circulate a church DVD on which a range of congregation members talk about their faith and the church, and on which clips of church services and events are shown. The overall message is not 'Come and join our organization and become a treasurer or secretary of something', but 'We are on a spiritual journey, like you are, come and relate with us as we go on our journey together.'

Leaflet drop invitations can still be effective, but be aware of the sheer amount of material that drops through letterboxes these days. The general experience is that people respond well to Christmas invitations but usually not at other times of the year. It may be that the best policy in many churches is to concentrate on a high-quality Christmas mailing and on one other at a different time of year when there is something especially attractive to invite people to.

Finally, it is usually a good policy to get on good terms with the local press and radio. Appoint a church member as press officer and let them offer stories from time to time – not so many that they are too trivial and just bore the press, but just enough so that the church becomes known as a regular source of column inches. Getting in news stories (especially with a good picture) generates good free publicity and is much better than adverts with service times, which cost money and hardly ever seem to result in people turning up.

Session 1 checklists

Session 1: Discover				
Making the church more visible				
1 Personal contacts				
Questions	**Yes/Good** 3 points	**OK/ Satisfactory** 2 points	**Could be better** 1 point	**No/Poor** 0 points	**Total points**
1 Are you in touch with non-churchgoers?					
2 Are the people you know mainly sympathetic to church rather than antagonistic?					
3 Are at least some of your contacts local, not too far away to realistically invite?					
4 How easy would you personally find it to invite someone to come to church?					
5 If your minister asked all regular church attenders to invite someone to 'Back to Church Sunday' do you think most people would do so?					
6 Does your church have a variety of services and events to invite non-churchgoers to?					
Your Score out of 18 =					

An average score of 12 or more suggests your church is doing pretty well in this area. Under 12, and you might want to revisit your answers to see where improvements might be made in this general area. Any individual item scoring 1 or 0 may also need highlighting for improvement.

Who is your first priority to invite to an event and what sort of event would be appropriate?

Session 1: Discover
Making the church more visible

2 Church programme

Questions	Yes/Good 3 points	OK/ Satisfactory 2 points	Could be better 1 point	No/Poor 0 points	Total points
1 Does your church have a programme that is open and attractive to the whole community?					
2 If you have a hall, do non-churchgoers use it?					
3 Do people in need turn to your church for help?					
4 Do congregation members go out of their way to befriend hall-users and other contacts?					
5 Are fund-raising events in your church mainly about meeting people rather than taking their money?					
6 Does your programme keep making new contacts?					
7 Is your programme small enough to be done well?					
8 Is it easy for people to progress from attending an event in the hall or church to attending services?					
9 Could your church turn an existing event into 'church' for those who come?					
10 Is there a culture of inviting contacts to church services and nurture courses?					
Your Score out of 30 =					

An average score of 20 or more suggests your church is doing pretty well in this area. Under 20, and you might want to revisit your answers to see where improvements might be made in this general area. Any individual item scoring 1 or 0 will also need highlighting for improvement.

How do you think your church programme might be made more inviting?

Session 1: Discover

31

Session 1: Discover
Making the church more visible

3 Special services

Questions	Yes/Good 3 points	OK/ Satisfactory 2 points	Could be better 1 point	No/Poor 0 points	Total points
1 Is there a range of Christmas services that attract non-churchgoers?					
2 Do you have other regular or one-off special services throughout the year?					
3 Do congregation members make good contact with those who come for baptisms, weddings and funerals?					
4 Do lots of congregation members attend the special services?					
5 Are attractive invitations to your normal services given out at the special services?					
6 Are individuals who attend special services followed up and befriended?					
7 Do you take part in 'Back to Church Sunday' and do your congregation members actually bring people?					
Your Score out of 21 =					

An average score of 14 or more suggests your church is doing pretty well in this area. Under 14, and you might want to revisit your answers to see where improvements might be made in this general area. Any individual item scoring 1 or 0 may also need highlighting for improvement.

What would be the two most effective changes your church could make to increase the chances of people finding their way from special services into regular attendance?

1

2

Session 1: Discover
Making the church more visible

4 Premises and publicity

Questions	Yes/Good 3 points	OK/ Satisfactory 2 points	Could be better 1 point	No/Poor 0 points	Total points
1 Can your church be found on the web?					
2 Do you have an informative web site, regularly updated?					
3 Is it easy to find out your service times without going to look at the notice board?					
4 Does the notice board look attractive and contemporary?					
5 Is your notice board up to date and informative?					
6 Does the church widely distribute a magazine or equivalent around the area?					
7 Does the church widely circulate attractive invitations to Christmas services?					
8 Does the church ever have positive coverage in the local media?					
9 Does the church make personal testimonies available, e.g. on a DVD?					
10 Does the church have any sort of 'newcomers' pack' to give to people who may try you out?					
Your Score out of 30 =					

An average score of 20 or more suggests your church is doing pretty well in this area. Under 20, and you might want to revisit your answers to see where improvements might be made in this general area. Any individual item scoring 1 or 0 may also need highlighting for improvement.

What would be the single most effective improvement to the way you inform people about your church and encourage them to try it?

Session 1: Discover

The premises

Session 2

Making them more inviting

■ Contents ■

■ Session 2 aim ■

The aim of this session is to review the messages given out to strangers and newcomers by the plant and facilities of the church. It also aims to review the attitudes that shape the plant and facilities. The session should enable church members to shape their personal contributions and to identify general priorities for creating a truly welcoming environment.

■ Session 2 outline ■

Exercise on arrival Seeing the building with new eyes
followed by a 5 minute break before the start of the session .... **allow up to 30 minutes**

Welcome Housekeeping notices and prayer .... 3 minutes

DVD Introduction Getting worried about anxiety and **Out and about: Photos of unwelcoming churches** .... 3 minutes

Word on welcome Reading: Matthew 21.12-16 with brief comment .... 6 minutes

Strangers' report How welcoming they find your premises? .... 8 minutes

DVD Customer care in the church Mark Hope-Urwin compares customer care in the retail sector and church .... 7 minutes

What did you notice? Those who tried to see the building with new eyes before the session started report what they saw.................................... 8 minutes

Checklists Exterior and entrance; worship space; social space: special needs – fill in, discuss in pairs or groups and hand in......................... 35 minutes

DVD How do they do that? How churches can make their buildings welcoming during the week .... 8 minutes

So what did we learn? Sharing ideas and conclusions, announcing checklist results .... 10 minutes

DVD Authors' conclusion What are you going to do? .... 1 minute

Course Prayer .... 1 minute

■ Session 2 leaders' notes ■

Getting the feel of it

Here are a couple of ideas for preparatory small group work:

1 Ask a range of small groups to list the five aspects of the buildings that matter most to them (heating, chairs, etc. etc.). Collect together in a plenary session to see how much agreement there is. Should they then be your priorities?

2 Invite people with different disabilities to speak about their particular issues with your building. Get a wheelchair-user to give a running commentary while negotiating their way around the building. Do this sensitively and seriously!

A report on either of these could be given during Session 2 in the 'what did you notice?' section. Or someone such as a wheelchair user could give their commentary live during the session.

Exercise on arrival This session should take place in the usual worship space. As people arrive ask them to wander around trying to pretend this is their first time in the building. Give them a piece of paper and a pen and ask them to jot down the main things that occur to the. Have a box available in which they can post their comments and also say that there will be a chance for them to report back in the training session.

Welcome Make it warm! Use the Course Prayer

DVD Introduction Getting worried about anxiety and **Out and about: Photos of unwelcoming churches**. The introduction asks course members to become more aware of the anxiety feelings our buildings may generate. The photo sequence shows how off putting many exteriors and notice boards are – their main messages being 'keep out' and 'closed down'. Things are not always this bad, of course, but it did not take the photographer long to find them!

Word on welcome Have someone read Matthew 21.12-16 and make a very brief comment on it. This is not an excuse for a sermon! The comment should be along the lines:

> Notice how passionately Jesus felt about the Temple as a house of prayer. Even though he had come to bring temple worship to an end through his own sacrifice once and for all for the sins of the world, the environment and ambience of the place where people came to meet with God was still important to him. So he got rid of the clutter and of the money-changers but he was also changing the atmosphere of the place – suddenly it became a place of healing and prayer and of happy shouting children. The physical environment and the inner attitudes of the people are interrelated.

Strangers' report Ask one or two genuine strangers to look round the premises a few days before Session 2 and now invite them briefly to report their reactions to the group. The strangers should ideally be non-churchgoers, although folk from a nearby church might be equally helpful. If the strangers are nervous of being critical in a meeing their comments could be written down and circulated or read out.

DVD Customer care in the church Mark Hope-Urwin's spent years as an award-winning customer care manager, and he has a very interesting angle on customer care in churches. Perhaps he'll convince you that your church needs a customer care manager!

What did you notice? People who tried the 'looking with new eyes' exercise before the training sesion began (or did it at some other time) should have been invited to write down their observations and hand them in. But at this point give them also a few minutes to report on anything they thought was particularly important. Do not let one person dominate – try to get very short, crisp contributions from several people.

Checklists As the introductory material ranges over all four of today's aspects and as people have now had some experience of filling in the checklists, we are asking course members to score all four lists in one go this time. We suggest that you encourage people to fill in all four, mainly going on gut instinct. There will then be time for course members to compare notes in twos or threes or fours and perhaps to look at the discussion questions at the end of each list. Just before the end of the time the lists should be gathered in so that the compilation work is undertaken as the last DVD clip is shown. Find four people, each one adding up the scores of one of the four checklists, and you should find you have results to announce before the end of the evening.

DVD How do they do that? To be shown while the checklist results are being compiled. This session has concentrated on how to make people feel welcome to events and services. But it is also important to make church buildings welcoming and accessible to visitors during the week. In some churches there are more people who pray in them on private visits during the week than in the formal services on a Sunday. This clip should stimulate thinking in this area.

So what did we learn? Start by asking a few groups or pairs what has struck them most in this session. Announce the average scores for each checklist, perhaps also announcing any individual questions that got an exceptionally low or high mark. Focus on two questions:

1 What are the main strengths of our buildings and equipment? How can we consolidate them?

2 What are the main problem areas? What can we do about them in the short term without spending a lot of money and in the longer term using rather more money?

In a larger group you may want sheets of paper handed out with these two questions on for written responses to go along with the verbal ones. Someone should make a note of all the points raised in this last session.

DVD Authors' conclusion As well as suggesting implications for church policy this also challenges individuals to make a personal contribution to improving welcome. Finish with **Course Prayer**.

Time-saving tips There should be time for the whole programme providing that the leader keeps a sharp eye on timing. However, it should be possible to reduce the time needed for checklists by cutting short the groups discussion time. Also you could miss out 'what did we notice?' or else simply read out a few of the comments handed in at the start of the session.

Session 2 pre-reading

This is a whole session about your plant and buildings, about the general environment and ambience of worship. These things are very important to our welcome. The standard of hospitality on offer to newcomers really does help determine whether they have a good experience and are likely to return. However, there is a danger. The human welcome and relationships are more important – a good human welcome can override poor premises and a poor human welcome can immediately cancel out the hard-won gain of good premises. So do be careful that your course members do not only focus on buildings because doing something about them is less threatening than focusing on their own human attitudes and behaviour. And we think you will find that the human engagement can't really be dissociated from the environment the humans create, so this is actually not just a nuts and bolts session.

The course notes below are designed to introduce each of the four checklists in turn and it is important to encourage all course members to read them in the week prior to the session. They will not be repeated on the DVD. Much of the DVD material will be delivered very entertainingly by Mark Hope-Urwin, who, until recently, was customer care manager for a large, well-known store. His insights are fascinating, helpful and humorous. As he ranges over the whole subject we have put all of the four personal checklists at the end of this session.

In Session 1 we established that some people will come to experience your church's worship for the first time because of a contact made through the church's programme and ministries, or because they belong to a group that hires out the premises during the week, or through some other community contact. Other people will come first to a special event or service such as a baptism, wedding, funeral, memorial service, Christmas, Mothering Sunday, Harvest, church parade or 'Back to Church Sunday'. Yet others will come through a personal contact, perhaps of the clergy but usually as friends or family of church members. Finally, some will find out about the church through the web site or notice board or church magazine, or literature that has been distributed. Some of these people will be experienced churchgoers, some will not have been for years, perhaps since Sunday school, and others will be totally new to churchgoing.

✳For whatever reason, and by whatever route, new people do turn up for worship events in most of our churches. Experience and research suggest that very few of those who 'try us out' actually stick and become regular congregation members themselves. When it comes to people who turn up for baptisms, weddings, funerals or carol services the percentage is nearly zero. How can we improve our welcome to worship so that more of the people who try attending end up belonging?

There are two main dimensions to the initial experience of worship, whether it is in a traditional service or building or in some sort of fresh expression or unusual setting. One dimension is physical and the other is human – in other words, how welcoming is the environment of worship and how welcoming are the people the newcomer worships with? Session 2 is about the easy bit – the environment – and looks in turn at four main aspects:

1 Exterior and entrance

2 Worship space

3 Kitchen and social space

4 Provision for people with special needs

In all of this the trick is to see ourselves as others see us – this could be scary!

1 Exterior and entrance

Many of our churches have had attention, love and money lavished on them so that they are attractive, welcoming buildings set in lovely grounds. They feel like a second home to us if we worship in them regularly but how do they seem to a newcomer?

One church had its grounds full of shrubs – vastly overgrown. The new vicar got a working party to clear the grounds and make lawns. One local resident was heard to say, 'It's good to see it's open. We thought it had closed down.'

> **Over to you ...**
>
> Compare your local church with a high street shop, pub or restaurant.
>
> Go and stand outside some of them. How do you judge them from the outside? What makes you want to go in? Look at how much money they spend on making the entrance bright and attractive. Why do they think this is money well spent? How does your church compare?

The Diocese of Lichfield held a competition for the 'Worst Notice Board in the Diocese'. The prize was a new notice board. There were some spectacularly bad entries – if a shop had signage like that it would certainly get no customers. We'll show you some examples on the screen in Session 2. How good is your notice board?

I asked some church members what they thought of their church notice board. 'No idea' was the general answer – 'We never look at it', 'Do we have one, where is it?'

Actually it was very unhelpful, containing hardly any information about the church and its services. But they didn't bother to check when they walked past it every week because they already knew the time and style of their own service and how to get hold of the vicar.

Sometimes we just don't see what sticks out a mile to an outsider.

Divine Inspiration: Helen McGowan and Janet Sewell

2 Worship space

Are you worried about anxiety?

You have interpreted the notice board correctly and negotiated the church path. You have pushed open the church door and taken a step inside. What do you find then?

Do you emerge into an entrance hall or foyer dimly lit, smelling of something nameless, cluttered with stuff no one is brave enough to take to the tip and without clear directions to the next stage of the obstacle course called 'going to church'? Or do

Mark Hope-Urwin

you walk straight into a warm, clean, well-lit worship space to be greeted by a smiling human being?

Buildings generate anxiety levels in people. A department store is trying all the time to make people feel good about being there – to lower the anxiety level.

Anxiety levels are raised by:

- uncertainty – where do I go, what do I do when I don't really know the house rules?
- clutter – feeling hemmed in, having to avoid it, being afraid of knocking something over
- feelings of not fitting in – I'm overdressed or underdressed for this environment, this is too posh or too down market for me
- smells, grot, litter, evidence of neglect, mystery, discomfort, dim lights, uneven floors, cold, lack of good signage or of provision for non-standard people – short-sighted, deaf, blind, short, tall, bad backs, weak bladders, English as second language etc. etc.
- unfamiliarity – 'I've never been in a place like this before', or 'It looks like a set from a horror movie.'
- staff who do not smile and do not offer to help.

A department store wants people to feel relaxed so they will enjoy spending their money and will want to come back again. A good customer-care manager will constantly patrol the store in order to root out anything that raises anxiety levels. Assistants will ask people consulting the store guide whether they can help them find what they are looking for and they will take them to the appropriate department and introduce them to an appropriate sales assistant. Staff who deal with the public will be hired and fired on the basis not of their skill level but on the basis of their attitude. Could your church do with a customer-care manager?

> ## Over to you ...
>
> Does entering your church building raise anxiety levels in people who are not familiar with it? Ask around and chat to your friends. Try and identify in your mind any features that particularly raise anxiety levels. Next time you go in make a note of how it makes you feel.
>
> What can be done to lower anxiety levels?

OK – so you are new and you have made it inside the building for a service. You have received a bucketful of books and papers from the welcomer or sidesperson. He or she may not have told you what to do next but you have correctly guessed that you are expected to sit down on a pew or chair. Wisely, you sit near the back so that you do not stick out like a sore thumb with everyone else's eyes studying the back of your neck and trying to guess why on earth you have come.

What is the building going to do to you over the next hour or so?

Is the church well lit so that the average 70-year-old can easily read the print in the order of service? And what about the print, whether in books, notice sheets or on the screen – is it big and clear enough for almost everyone to read? And what allowance is made for people who cannot read very well? They become adept at hiding their problem and will probably not return to a church that makes them look a fool if they can't read long words fluently.

Is the church warm enough in winter so that people do not steadily cool down as they listen to the sermon? Are the newcomers in shirt sleeves and the regulars in fur coats? Remember that most people today dress all the time for centrally heated rooms and cars. Some do not even possess any warm clothing.

You may realize that the heating system installed five years ago is no better than the old one out of the Ark but that is no comfort to the newcomer who came without a thick jersey. Is the old reassurance that 'Many are cooled but few are frozen' actually good enough in this day and age?

In one church they made sure the heater by the door was fully on to give everyone a good impression when they came in, but the rest were turned down to save money, so everyone shivered – and the warden had set the heating to go off halfway through the service!

In another church, when the warden died, they found that he had superglued the thermostat inside the boiler casing so no matter what you did with the dial it was still set on 'low'!

One church had to have the heating on for 36 hours to really heat the place and prevent down draughts that turned the pages for you. When they began to do this it was a great investment because people came, stayed – and *paid*! Another church building leaked so much heat it could not be warmed properly in winter. The congregation was dwindling. The vicar persuaded the church members to use the (warm) church hall for worship in the winter and attendance quickly rose from 70 to 90.

Is the seating comfortable and attractive? Pew enthusiasts please consider whether you sit by choice on hard wooden benches in your living room at home and expect your guests to do the same! I recently spent some time helping Anglican churches in Australia think about how to grow. I sat in about ten churches and, having a slightly bad back, I concluded that I could not have joined any of these churches because in every one the wooden pews mangled my back. My sister came to my own church one Sunday in the days before we got rid of the pews. It was a healing service and she had a bad back. But when the time came for people to go up to be prayed for, the pew had done for her – she couldn't move!

Do newcomers run the risk of sitting in some regular's place and offending them? Is there any risk of the newcomer being told to move? One couple I knew came to a midweek service and were 'asked to move' three times! They refused to come back. I told the congregation that if that couple lost faith, then on Judgement Day they would have to face God with what they had done. But if they ever did it again they would have to face me first!

Is there a good-quality sound system such that everyone can hear the leader, the preacher, the notices, the music group leader's introductions etc.? Is the sound level of the organ or the music group about right? Remember that the big amplification that excites younger ears can be painful to older ones. If people's voices are drowned out either by the organ or the band they will stop trying to compete.

If there is a data projector and screen, are they of professional quality and is the screen visible from every seat? If there is no projector and screen, have you considered their advantages? People no longer have to locate hymn numbers in books, they sing looking up not down, the worship can flow from one song to another, you can use video clips and sermon illustrations, the screen can welcome people and give simple instructions for the service ahead to lower anxiety levels before the service begins. Not so many people read books these days, but everyone is used to watching a screen. But please train the operator to change slides at the right time! Insiders may know the start of the next verse but strangers don't! A three-second delay is a great way to confuse and discourage them.

If there are hymn and service books, are they attractive and clean, and easy to use?

Is there a notice sheet that makes you proud to be a member of this community?

Several of the Australian churches I visited recently did not even have a toilet on the premises. I think that will increasingly worry me as I get older. It would certainly have worried me when our children were young! 'What are we doing wrong?' asked one local church. 'We do everything right but the young families never stick with us.' They were expecting a sophisticated reply from the church growth expert. 'They won't stick until you get a toilet', I replied.

Are the signs to the toilet clear and visible to all and are the toilets clean, and easily accessible without an embarrassing walk along the edge of the communion rail? Are there enough toilets so that there is no queue when the newcomer is likely to need them? Are there baby-change facilities and wheelchair access?

Then what about the way in which the building and its interior connect you with God, or at least calm you down and enable you to be in touch spiritually? The architecture of the internal space can depress or excite, lift you to the heavens or make you miserable. Some people respond spiritually to ancient Gothic buildings that have been prayed in for centuries. For others these are a turn-off and what they need is a human-scale hall. It is interesting that, usually, when a congregation has to leave its specialized church building for a few months for re-ordering or repairs, congregation numbers grow. They return to normal when the building is reoccupied. What dynamic is going on there?

Is it easy to pray in your worship space? Does it feel prayed in and loved? What do the wall hangings, the statues, the communion table, the altar, candles, kneelers, stained-glass windows, pulpit, or the cross over the archway do for you? Are there places in the church where you feel psychologically comfortable sitting and others where you are not so comfy? Do you all leave those less-favoured places for the strangers?

3 Kitchen and social space

So, at long last the service is over and you are invited to refreshments. This is the last and greatest hurdle of them all ...

Getting there is half the battle

The first issue is whether you know that refreshments are available, whether you know where to go to get them and whether you have been invited. It certainly helps if the service leader has invited you in the notices. But the most important invitation is personal – if a regular invites you to join them for coffee you are likely to go, if not you are much more likely to slip away without talking to people. In many churches newcomers are genuinely welcomed to refreshments at the end, but not everywhere!

I visited one church that had seen rapid attendance decline. I enquired about their refreshments policy. 'Oh, we only serve refreshments to the regulars when the others have gone', came the reply. The warden indicated a secret area behind a curtain at the back of the church. 'The new people just shake hands with the vicar on the way out.'

So are your newcomers genuinely made to feel welcome to refreshments and conversation at the end of a service?

If refreshments are served very close to the worship area within the same building, more people will join in than if they are served in a church hall a short walk away going outdoors. So are you serving refreshments in the right place and, if not, what can be done about it?

Some churches still don't even serve refreshments at all, and the people don't stick around after the service. I once became vicar of a church where one large congregation never served refreshments and it was always a race out of the door after the blessing. I soon discovered that the people did not really even know each other, even though some of them had been worshipping with each other for decades. They did not even know each other's names. There was no community to invite newcomers to belong to, and there was no hope of the regulars welcoming the newcomers if they did not even talk to each other. We installed a refreshment area and new toilets, we started serving coffee, people stayed and things got a lot friendlier!

But what do you do if your church is very small and you have no realistic chance of installing a kitchen? You may need to remove the back pew to create a circulating space and to install a bench on which to boil a kettle and put out some attractive biscuits. One church made the furniture for their new refreshment point out of the back pew timber – neat eh! Or folk could bring large flasks of hot water. There is always a way if there is a will.

Service and salmonella

So let's now have a look at the state of the kitchen. Is it clean, modern, hygienic, well designed for largish-scale catering, with plenty of space and no health and safety issues? Are you legally allowed to sell food to the public from it? When was it last inspected? Or is it the sort your grandma used to have, except now encrusted with the spillages and rustiness of the ages? Is there a constricted serving hatch that generates a huge queue just for a cup of tea? In short, would you be happy if the church kitchen were your own kitchen at home?

The content of refreshments offered is very important. In an age where tastes have become sophisticated and quality assumed as a right, too many churches still offer bottom-of-the-range coffee and biscuits, and many even charge for them. Any church that is serious about welcome and hospitality will have a budget for refreshments and offer them for free. The drinks will be high quality and fairly traded. The food will also be enticing. There is fairly traded food around these days as well as drinks. The acid test is – would you be proud to offer these refreshments to your guests at home and would you be pleased to receive them as a guest in someone else's home?

It was 'Back to Church Sunday' at St Agatha's. Guests had come and the church had gone to town with the biscuits – top of the range instead of the usual chocolate-free, rich-tea zone. A visitor really fancied a chocolate biscuit and asked for one at the hatch. 'I'm sorry, they've been very popular and they've all gone,' said the serving lady, 'I had to save mine on the side here.' Which all goes to prove it is easier to solve the physical problems of the building than the human ones!

Happy children bring their parents again

What happens after the service can be a major part of the experience for children as well as adults. Think through what refreshments are offered to the children to make them feel special and want to come again. Is the aim to save money on their refreshments or to make the children happy? And if the church is still offering junk food what are the healthy options to move towards?

By and large, at the end of a service children prefer to play with each other rather than stand around a hall listening to adults gossip. Is there somewhere for them to go and something for them to do? In one church I built a model railway that came out to be played with when the church service was over. And we had a balcony from which we held paper aeroplane competitions using old notice sheets. And we let the smaller children play with the drum kit provided they didn't hit it too hard! What is there in your church to make the children feel at home and want to return because they feel welcomed and special and have fun? It may also be a good idea to create an area where the children can display their craftwork from the children's groups. Certainly make sure there is good quality children's artwork on the walls. The church I was at the other week brought out the table tennis table at the end of the service and I much preferred playing with the teenagers to standing around being polite with the adults!

Our health and safety culture has its idiocies but also its common-sense good points. So how safe is your church, your kitchen, your social space, your church path and car park and grounds? If parents spot sharp points protruding from old metal chairs, or dangerously hot radiators, or broken glass, or plain honest dirt, or any one of a number of other potential dangers, they may not bring their tiny tots again. If they are nervous about fire precautions and evacuation procedures, they will also be reluctant to return.

A well-cared-for, safe, high-quality environment for refreshments, socializing and playtime is no substitute for welcoming human beings. But they don't half help!

4 Provision for people with special needs

Special needs have cropped up from time to time already. Making provision for people with them is not a matter of offering optional extras for small minorities but of maintaining the essential features of a welcoming church.

My Mum was 96 and couldn't see as well as she used to. Churchgoing was stressful for her because she couldn't read the words in most hymn books and join in properly. One Sunday friends took her to a different church and she asked the door welcomer for a large-print hymn book. 'We can do better than that', he said, giving her the full order of service including all the liturgy, hymns and notices in a really clear large print folder. She could join in with no trouble and loved the welcome she had been given.

Most of us do not have to wait until we are 96 to have some sort of special need or weakness that makes a significant difference to our experience of the worship event. Here is a far from exhaustive list:

- Bad back – I put this first because it's personal!
- Hard of hearing
- Find loud noises from organs or music groups distressing
- Deaf
- Need reading glasses and find small print hard
- Colour blind
- Blind or partially sighted

- Wobbly on feet, use a stick, elderly
- Wheelchair user
- Disabled badge holder
- Not fully confident of the bladder (applies to the very young as well as to elderly people)
- Bald – in trouble from those overhead radiant heaters some churches have unthinkingly installed (this too is personal!)
- Food allergies
- Recovering alcoholic (communion wine problems)
- Need to breast-feed
- Tabloid-only reader
- Illiterate
- English as second language
- Little or no English
- Very short – mainly but not exclusively children
- Very tall
- Overweight – some pew spaces and chairs are embarrassingly inadequate for what is known in church circles as 'the wider community'
- Dodgy knees – to kneel or not to kneel, that is the question
- Short attention spans – mainly applies to children but to plenty of others as well!

Catering for people with different needs means we can have lots of people with different needs coming along.

I met Fred at the hospital where his wife was dying: both of them were profoundly deaf. I was a useless chaplain but gave them my card. Elsie died and two weeks later Fred came to church with an interpreter. We had to make room and allow the service to be interrupted. The following week he brought two friends and the following week two more (all deaf). The interpreter and his wife both became Christians, and trained over 20 others to sign for all the deaf people who had joined our congregation because we had provided for their needs.

> **Over to you ...**
>
> **If you think about it then probably the majority of your congregation have some sort of special physical need or issue that affects their church experience. On the list above tick any that affect you or perhaps a friend of yours and add any others at the bottom of the list. How well does your church cater for your special need and how could it improve? If you have a suggestion or request to make, write it down and take it with you to Session 2. Hand it in to the course leader.**

Session 2: The premises

Session 2 checklists

Session 2: The premises
Making them more inviting

1 Exterior and entrance

Questions	Yes/Good 3 points	OK/ Satisfactory 2 points	Could be better 1 point	No/Poor 0 points	Total points
1 Is your church's location one people feel safe walking to?					
2 Is there a good, clear, safe route from the pavement and car park?					
3 Is there good quality car parking, adequate for normal usage?					
4 Are the grounds and graveyard well kept and attractive?					
5 Is it obvious which door gets you into the building and is the signage clear?					
6 Is your church door easy to use at service times?					
7 Can you see through the door or is it forbidding, like a prison door?					
8 Is there good access for those who use wheelchairs and partially sighted people?					
9 Does your building provoke feelings of awe, wonder and a sense of God?					
10 Overall, how good is the experience of walking into church for the first time?					
			Your Score out of 30 =		

An average score of 20 or more suggests your church is doing pretty well in this area. Under 20, and you might want to revisit your answers to see where improvements might be made in this general area. Any individual item scoring 1 or 0 may also need highlighting for improvement.

What do you think your church can do about any specific issues?

a cheaply in the short term?

b more expensively in the long term?

Session 2: The premises
Making them more inviting

2 The worship space

Questions	Yes/Good 3 points	OK/ Satisfactory 2 points	Could be better 1 point	No/Poor 0 points	Total points
1 Is the church lighting good enough for reading?					
2 Is the church heating effective and will the visitor be comfortable?					
3 Is the church seating comfy and back-friendly?					
4 Are there clear signs for the church toilets?					
5 Are the sound system and hearing loop clear and not overpowering?					
6 Are the books, leaflets and notice sheets or projector and screen clear and good quality?					
7 Are minority groups and people with special needs well provided for?					
8 Is the building tidy and uncluttered?					
9 Do the furniture and fittings (e.g. altar cross, wall hangings) draw you to God?					
10 Is the general feel of the place 'warm'?					
Your Score out of 30 =					

An average score of 20 or more suggests your church is doing pretty well in this area. Under 20, and you might want to revisit your answers to see where improvements might be made in this general area. Any individual item scoring 1 or 0 may also need highlighting for improvement.

What do you think your church can do about any specific issues?

a   cheaply in the short term?

b   more expensively in the long term?

Session 2: The premises

49

Session 2: The premises
Making them more inviting

3 The social space

Questions	Yes/Good 3 points	OK/ Satisfactory 2 points	Could be better 1 point	No/Poor 0 points	Total points
1 Are the refreshments close at hand and obvious?					
2 Is the hall or social space attractive and well cared for?					
3 Is the kitchen clean and hygienic rather than a mess?					
4 Does the refreshment system have easy access rather than a long queue?					
5 Are the refreshments appetizing and attractive rather than cheap and nasty?					
6 Are the refreshments free rather than a donation being asked for?					
7 Are children offered good and appropriate refreshments?					
8 Do children have good facilities and play options rather than being bored while adults chat to each other?					
9 Does it look like health and safety issues have been addressed?					
Your Score out of 27 =					

An average score of 18 or more suggests your church is doing pretty well in this area. Under 18, and you might want to revisit your answers to see where improvements might be made in this general area. Any individual item scoring 1 or 0 may also need highlighting for improvement.

What do you think your church can do about any specific issues?

a   cheaply in the short term?

b   more expensively in the long term?

Session 2: The premises
Making them more inviting

4 Provision for people with special needs

Is provision made for	Yes/Good 3 points	OK/ Satisfactory 2 points	Could be better 1 point	No/Poor 0 points	Total points
1 … those who are deaf or hard of hearing?					
2 … wheelchair users?					
3 … parking for disability scooters?					
4 … elderly people unsteady on their feet?					
5 … dealing with distressed, difficult people?					
6 … food allergies?					
7 … those with alcohol problems (e.g. non-alcoholic wine)?					
8 … partially sighted or blind people?					
9 … poor readers?					
10 … those for whom English is a second language?					
Your Score out of 30 =					

An average score of 20 or more suggests your church is doing pretty well in this area. Under 20, and you might want to revisit your answers to see where improvements might be made in this general area. Any individual item scoring 1 or 0 may also need highlighting for improvement.

What is the most urgent and relevant issue to tackle in your church?

A welcoming God
and his welcoming people

■ Contents ■

■ Session 3 aim ■

The aim of this session is to review the suitability and attractiveness of church services for newcomers and strangers. It should reveal priorities for corporate change, and help individual church members to be God's welcoming people more effectively.

■ Session 3 outline ■

Welcome Housekeeping notices and prayer .... 3 minutes

DVD Introduction A friendly church? and **Out and about:
Finding the God moments** .... 4 minutes

Word on welcome Reading: James 2.1-10 with brief comments .... 6 minutes

DVD What mystery worshippers say .... 7 minutes

Our mystery worshippers A report from those who attended your own
church as mystery worshippers .... 6 minutes

DVD How do they do that? Interview with Tim Lomax about worship
that works .... 7 minutes

Checklists Initial welcome; worship experience; children and teens;
after the service – fill in, discuss in pairs or groups and hand in .... 35 minutes

True story A church member tells the story of how they met a welcoming
God and his welcoming people when they first started coming to church .... 5 minutes

So what did we learn? What have we learnt from the checklists
(announce the results)? What are our strengths, weaknesses and
opportunites for change? .... 15 minutes

DVD Authors' conclusion People will join a church if they meet a
welcoming people and are helped to encounter the living God .... 1 minute

Course Prayer .... 1 minute

■ Session 3 leaders' notes ■

Getting the feel of it

Here are three ideas for preparatory small group work:

1 Divide into small groups and ask each group to list the top five emotions people feel when in a new environment. What can help to make the emotions more positive? Ask each group to select and share their reflections on a specific emotion with the other groups.

2 Give each small group a very brief thumbnail sketch of a different kind of newcomer (e.g. young/old, no faith/mature Christian). Ask them to work out what their newcomer might find most helpful by way of welcome into the church community.

3 Ask people to pair off. One person feigns ignorance of the church and the other one has to explain what happens in a normal church service moment by moment. This should show up how much we take for granted.

A brief report on any one of these could be given during Session 3, either alongside the mystery worshipper report or in the 'true story' slot.

DVD Introduction A friendly church? and **Out and about: Finding the God moments** This introduces the twin themes that people will join a church community and become disciples if they are offered human friendship and meet the living God.

Word on welcome Have someone read James 2.1-10 and comment briefly on it, along these lines:

> One way of loving your neighbours as yourself is to offer the sort of welcome to newcomers into church that we would wish to receive ourselves. The title of this whole course is 'EVERYBODY Welcome'. It looks like the early churches were tempted to welcome the rich and respectable more warmly than the poor and disreputable. Are there ways in which we perhaps subconsciously grade our welcome according to the external appearance of the newcomer? How can we give the best possible welcome to everybody and so fulfil the royal law found in Scripture, to 'Love your neighbour as yourself'?

DVD What mystery worshippers say Mystery worshippers reveal some of the things they have found when visiting church services. This should get your church members thinking about their own church. They should be re-assured that, if there are problems in their own church, they are not alone. On the other hand news of good practice is always inspiring.

Our mystery worshippers Hopefully you were able to arrange for mystery worshippers to attend your church on the quiet a few weeks ago. Perhaps they were professional 'mystery shoppers' or friends doing you a favour, or Christians from another church. Details of how to go about 'mystery worshipping' are found on the course website **www.everybodywelcome.org.uk**. If they are brave enough ask them to give a verbal report or else circulate or read out something written down. It is helpful if the mystery worshippers are present but not essential. Do not allow a situation to develop where church members get defensive and start an argument with the mystery worshipper by trying to justify themselves!

DVD How do they do that? This DVD shows clips of a service with a lot of congregational participation together with reflections on what helps different individuals have a spiritual experience and encounter God.

Initial welcome checklist Tell people that you are assuming they have read the Members' Manual for Session 3. Explain that this is not a referendum on how good your individual sidespeople or initial welcomers are. It is much more about the arrangements put in place by the whole church. Sidespeople should not feel got at, but rather that this is their chance to reflect on and to develop their ministry of welcome with the help of some feedback from other church members.

Worship experience checklist This is not a referendum on how good the vicar or anybody else is at leading worship. Rather it gives everyone a chance to reflect on the whole corporate experience and their part in it. Any leader of worship knows that the main determinant of how well things go is not their personal performance but the overall atmosphere and attitude of the whole people of God. If your congregation is made up of spiritual refrigerators you've no chance, if it's made up of spiritual radiators you're hardly needed.

Children and teens checklist Once again, this is not a referendum on how good your children's leaders are but rather a chance for honest reflection on how things are and how they could be better.

After service checklist Remind people that this is not primarily about how they feel at the end of a service but about how it feels to be new or a stranger at the end of a service in their church.

True story Only include this if you have someone suitable to ask. For preference they should be a fairly new church member. If you do not have someone suitable you could use the time to make a report on one of the 'getting the feel of it' exercises. Remember that part of the purpose of this 5-minute slot is to give the people counting the checklist scores some time to complete the task so you can announce results during the final discussion.

So what did we learn? Ask groups or individuals to say what they think is the main strength and then the main weakness of your church's welcome into the presence of God and the community of his people. What interesting differences in perception have the checklists thrown up? What are the main things that can be done to attend to the weaknesses and build on the strengths? There may be something in the short term that needs no decision-making process or budget and something in the long term that does.

DVD Authors' conclusion followed by **Course Prayer**

Time-saving tips We think that most churches will get through the programme in about an hour and a half, but if you are worried about timings because the previous sessions have overrun then you could make the mystery worshipper report into a written report handed to people as they arrive and just allow two minutes for reactions to it. Or, if your checklist counters are really efficient, you could go straight from the checklists to the final discussion and announce results half way through it.

Session 3 pre-reading

In Session 2 we considered the physical aspects of the church's 'Welcome to Worship' for newcomers. Here we turn to the even more important human aspects. Not only are these more important but also human behaviour is harder to change than physical buildings. The human side is more important because most people come to church in order to develop relationships – to build their relationship with God and to join a church community. Or if that isn't their motive, perhaps it should be! The human aspects are harder to change because, unlike buildings, human beings have a will of their own. However, the Christian faith is all about being changed and sanctified by God, so change is entirely possible and the rewards of change are great.

1 Initial welcome

The initial welcomer (sidesperson in Anglican churches, steward or usher in other churches) is a key person in the welcome ministry of the church. I have known many wonderful welcomers and the whole process in many churches is well managed. What a difference it makes! In some churches, traditionally the job of the initial welcomers is simply to hand out the hymn book, prayer book, order of service leaflet, notice sheet, the hymn book supplement for the hymn written in 1964, the invitation to the church weekend, the card with Easter services printed on, the extra sheet of paper with the really modern song written in 1988, and the appeal for funds to replace the clapped-out photocopier.

If possible, this great pile is landed on you without eye contact. In one church, resourceful sidespeople so positioned the table loaded with these goodies that their backs faced the entrance. They then perfected the art of handing the bundle to incoming worshippers backwards over their shoulders without at any time actually having to see their faces.

When I became vicar of a church in Sheffield I was bemused for the first few weeks by the fact that the sidespeople on duty were new every week and I had no idea who they were. Finally I discovered the church had found a way to attract non-members to come to church. They were put on the sidespeople's rota and turned up three times a year to welcome people in. In most churches the regulars welcomed the strangers. In this church it was the other way round.

But the role and significance of that first welcome is hard to overestimate. For a newcomer this is the moment of acutest anxiety. It is the moment of sitting in the dentist's chair, opening wide and seeing the drill descending. If the dentist is human, smiling and reassuring, if she explains what she is doing and tells you it won't hurt, then your anxiety level goes down. If she just comes at you with a drill, you panic.

The key point for sidespeople is that their main job is not to hand stuff out but to make people feel welcomed and at ease. If weather permits, it is a good idea to have one sidesperson outside, welcoming people before they set foot in the building. If it is raining let a couple of them wait on the church path with very large umbrellas. People who look unsure can then be accompanied in and shown the ropes. Those at a bit of a loss for where the entrance is, or who are having an attack of nerves, can be greeted and given confidence.

It is also a good idea to have enough folk on duty to spare one to accompany newcomers or people with particular needs to good seats and get them settled, to explain what is going to happen, to answer questions. If a newcomer is spotted, the sidesperson should know who in the congregation it is safe to sit them next to. 'Hello Sam, this is Joyce and Geoffrey, they're new so would you mind if they sit with you and you showed them the page numbers?'

Most people genuinely want to be welcomed, but a few individuals do not. They want their anonymity. But the fear of being too pushy, plus our natural shyness, paralyzes many of us and we become inert in the face of newcomers. Avoiding 'over-welcome' can be an excuse for not properly welcoming anyone. It is usually obvious if someone does not want warm human contact and it is important that among the initial welcomers there are people with enough sensitivity to spot them. But the general rule and the fall-back assumption must be that a warm and genuine initial welcome is a key stage in making people feel at home in church.

An elderly lady arrived at one church for the first time. The sidesperson shook her by the hand and said, 'Welcome to St Mary's.' The lady burst into tears and the sidesperson wondered what he had done wrong. After they had sat the lady down and dried her tears, she explained, 'That is the first time anyone has touched me for three years.' A simple human gesture had overwhelmed her. Do not underestimate the impact of human warmth and contact on the isolated and lonely victims of shattered communities and broken families who live all around us.

Many newcomers make an assessment of whether they stand a chance of joining a church within seconds of entering the door. There is one key question – 'Is there anyone like me?' It is important to have a range of people on the sidespersons' rota, and particularly a range of ages. If the aim is to attract families to this service then families should be on the front line of welcome. If teenagers, then teenagers should be the welcomers. If pensioners, then pensioners.

Some churches issue name badges to the initial welcomers. This identifies their role and helps newcomers relate to them – so their use should be encouraged. These can also be a way of finding out who visitors are. 'Hello, as you can see, my name is Richard, welcome to All Saints. I don't think we've met, have you been before?' is likely to elicit at least a name in response. That name should be committed to memory, written down and used again the very next time a newcomer returns.

How big should the rota of welcomers be? Most people today do not wish to be tied down every week, or even most weeks, to a regular job in a church. Perhaps an ideal mix is to have four or five teams all on once a month, but one or two people (perhaps an overall leader of the team) who will be ever-present and able to spot those who have already come once or twice.

What sort of people are we looking for to do this ministry? People who smile easily, are relaxed in company, and motivated not only to care for their fellow Christians but also to draw other people into the fellowship of the church and the love of God that they themselves value.

But what about the actual task of giving out the books? The welcomers should arrive early and have the piles of stuff all sorted before most people arrive. That way they can concentrate on the human relations. The table where the books are placed should not be behind the sidespeople so that their backs are to the people arriving when they sort and pick up the books. The table should not be between the sidespeople and the incoming worshippers as it then acts as a barrier. It should be to the side so that it is easy to shake hands and maintain eye contact throughout the initial welcome. If a table can be avoided altogether, so much the better.

It is preferable if there is actually very little to give out anyway. Dumping a pile of books and leaflets on a newcomer can so raise their anxiety levels right at the start that a large barrier has already been created. People are not used to finding hymn numbers or places in prayer books. In many, if not most, situations today it is better to have as much as possible on the screen from the data projector. A single attractive notice sheet is quite enough to give out and so give the opportunity for a warm human welcome to the worship event. If hymns and liturgies must be written out, it is usually worth the trouble of compiling them together in a single order of service that most strangers can follow reasonably easily.

2 The worship event

You the newcomer have found your way in, you have been welcomed by the sidespersons' team, you have found a seat. Now the service or fresh expression style of event is beginning. This is the heart of the matter. Will it be a mystery or turn-off to you or else an entry into a whole new spiritual world?

There is so much to say about this, the heart of the church we are welcoming people into, that it won't fit inside the Members' Manual. So you may need to help course members access the material below from the web site. Here is the 'over to you' exercise in the manual:

> **Over to you …**
>
> There is a web site associated with this course –
> **www.everybodywelcome.org.uk** When you have found it, click on
> 'worship event' and read all about it there! If you are not online then
> persuade someone to print off a copy for you. Or perhaps there may be
> copies available in church.

The standard of the football ground is important – is it clean and safe and comfortable? The behaviour of the crowd around you is also important – is it drunken and foul-mouthed or enthusiastic and happy? But what you have actually come for is the game and now the referee has blown the starting whistle. A dull, petulant 0–0 draw and you might decide you are not going to become a 'Rovers' fan. But an exciting, skilful 4–3 victory and you just might be hooked.

The team are waiting in the tunnel, ready for the signal to walk out onto the pitch. Every player waits expectantly, limbering up, jumping up and down and flexing their legs. Occasionally, a player shouts out encouragements, hoping to inspire his teammates. For the past week the team (players and coaches) have been hard at work putting tactics and skills into practice. Today is match day and the team are looking forward to giving their all, together in their own stadium, in front of the home fans.

'Active' worship

The referee signals and, to the accompanying music, the loud announcement over the PA system and the roar of the crowd, the players take to the pitch. Just how well preparations have been made is about to be put to the test. Will the team produce a world-class display – a thrilling end-to-end game or a dull-as-dish-water draw? Will the play be boring and predictable or flamboyant and eye-catching? Will the team display inspire every visitor in the stadium to pick up a ball and have a go? Will each player pull their weight and excel in their role? Will the game plan prove effective – how well will the team hold their shape and formation? When things go wrong, as they invariably do, will the players blame each other and argue among themselves? And what about the coaching staff; will they help the team realize their full potential? Only the team performance on the pitch will provide answers to these questions. How well the match goes and the subsequent result will, of course, directly impact the post-match drinks. The buzz of an exciting game will last well after the final whistle and energize many a conversation. It will also directly influence each player's future involvement in the team. No one really wants to play for a team going nowhere. Ask any player who they want to play for and they almost always give the answer: 'A team going places, a team with vision, a team with hopes and dreams, a team that wants me on their books.'

When we gather together for worship we are like members of a team taking to the pitch on match day. We each have an essential part to play in the worship offered. The aim: to give glory to God by enabling everyone to be active and fully involved team members, not passive spectators. In worship each of us has a vital and unique role (whether we lead from the front or not). We come with different gifts and talents, numerous learning styles, a diversity of backgrounds and stories, an array of hopes and dreams as well as very different struggles and fears. With all this diversity and difference we form a worshipping community.

Visitors and newcomers are an important part of this community. One of the aims of church worship is to help visitors and newcomers become spiritually alive as they are caught up in a collective experience of connecting God and humans. And as they become spiritually more alive within the worship of the church community they will become more bonded into it. So we hope and pray that every visitor will have a life-changing encounter with God's presence. But the things that are normal and relaxing to us may be strange and fearful to them. So how can we take care to usher in the newcomer to God's presence while not diluting the regulars' worship-encounter with the living Lord?

Or, to put the question another way, Irenaeus (a second-century bishop) tells us that the glory of God is a human fully alive. So, how well does our worship help those present to be fully alive? Does it inspire life and energy and vibrant community? Does it shape and transform us into Christ's living body? Does it connect with life, with culture? Does it challenge and provoke? Is it creative and imaginative? Will newcomers be attracted and engaged by the life and vibrancy of our worshipping community?

A community in which every member seeks to be fully alive will build its worship on the following principles:

Good leadership

Confidence and sincerity are the two keys. Prayerful preparation is the way to find them both. If there is an air of uncertainty in the leader, the congregation will tense and visitors will be uncomfortable. The leader should be familiar with the shape of the service and any liturgy being used. There should be no flapping of pages to locate obscure prayers or Bible verses, and no unintentional long pauses. Being well prepared does not mean a lack of reliance on the Holy Spirit – he can inspire our preparation as well as our delivery!

Eye contact and communication with conviction are also important. If other people are helping lead the service the main leader should check they know what they are doing – embarrassing slip-ups, pauses and confusions just raise anxiety levels in the congregation. But we don't need to pretend to be super-professional. If something goes wrong then it is best dealt with by a light remark that creates a ripple of laughter and punctures the tension.

At the start of the service it is important to offer both a warm welcome to all and an introduction to the service that explains its theme. Every service should be planned so that all the ingredients – the readings, the sermon, the prayers, the hymns etc. – 'work together for good'. So the leader should make sure that if there is indeed a theme, he or she is clear about it in their own mind and flag it up to the congregation. There is a delicate balance, though, between giving instructions and stage directions that are too intrusive and not giving them at all. So think through what areas are likely to be most difficult for newcomers and make sure that instructions are clear at those points. Some areas that are likely to induce anxiety among the less practised are:

■ Use of books and sheets. Give out page and hymn numbers and give people a few seconds to find them. It is of course very important to make life as easy as possible for newcomers by having no more than the barest essential in terms of page references – good use of projection and/or customized service sheets can avoid too many page turns and numbers.

- Children going out to their activity. Make sure people know when and how that is to happen.

- The Peace. If this is an issue in your church you may wish to devote a few minutes of course time to the art of sharing the peace with an uncomfortable stranger.

- Communion. This usually needs clear stage directions about the options available – come to receive, come for a blessing or stay put. It is all too easy to conjure up a loud 'no' from God by suggesting that certain people are not allowed to receive communion. Yet it is all too easy for an unconditional welcome to the body and blood of Christ to trivialize the sacrament. So it is best to say 'yes' to all by giving clear options that invite each individual to choose the one that holds the most integrity for them.

- The end of the service. Make sure people know what their options are and where refreshments are being offered. The Welcome Team and the whole congregation should ensure that every newcomer or visitor is put at their ease by a friendly face as the service ends.

Good structure

It is good that these days there is such variety of form and liturgy in our services. People encounter God in different ways and God is able to use every style of worship. All churches make use of a liturgical structure, however free they think they are being, and many have set liturgical texts. The important thing is neither to allow freedom to become a mess nor liturgy a straightjacket. Giving a visitor a clear road map for the service can give them security. If they haven't a clue what is going to happen next or how long the service is going to last their anxiety levels will rise.

Many screen-using churches already provide page numbers for hymns and songs (e.g. page 1 of 4) but this still leaves worshippers without a clear indication of service shape. The answer: provide a progress bar (for example, Gathering – Word – Sacrament – Dismissal in a communion service) at the top or bottom of each screen. The progress bar highlights the current point in the worship (Gathering – Word – Sacrament – Dismissal). Progress through the parts of a part of a service can also be highlighted, such as something along the lines of taking – thanking – breaking – sharing. This can be achieved quite simply using PowerPoint slides or by designing a template for the church presentation software. The progress bar is a simple but effective tool providing a basic map of the service, enabling worshippers to engage more fully in the worship journey.

Good sermons

People can easily switch off or drift away. Many people these days are not used to listening to a monologue. The correct response to this problem is not to preach a short sermon but a good one, not to preach a superficial sermon but a profound one, not to go off on theoretical flights of fancy, but to engage the listener in linking their everyday world to the God of the Bible. The sermon needs to be consistently good, so preparation should be a priority in the preacher's diary the week before. If someone is actually not very good at preaching, it is usually better to risk hurting them by asking them to step down than to risk hurting the congregation by allowing them to continue. All preachers need training, refresher training and leadership accountability to get the best out of them.

Good music

This can not only draw people into the heart of God but also attract people into coming back again. The quality of the music matters as much as the style, but the sincerity of the musicians matters the most. Church leaders will find that time, love and care invested in church musicians and singers is time well spent. But the musicians need a servant heart – they are not there to dictate what happens or to veto styles they don't personally like.

Too often the local church tries to produce in its weekly worship something it has seen elsewhere. This happens in all styles and traditions. What happens in a cathedral with a brilliant organist and trained choir cannot be replicated by a 95-year-old organist with three elderly choristers, one child and a cat. What happens at Spring Harvest with a ten-piece semi-professional band cannot be replicated on Joe's six-string with his son 'having a go' at the drums. Let's be realistic about our abilities and do the very best with what we have. Also, we need to be wary of too many unknown hymns or songs. At least 75 per cent of the hymns/songs chosen should be well known by the congregation so that they are sung well and the newcomer can join in. As a rule, never sing an unknown song or hymn at the beginning of a service; always start with something most people will know. There's nothing wrong with a new song or hymn but remember that to the newcomer most of them will be new and the only hope they have is that everyone else will at least be singing well so they can join in. If no one else is singing, there's nothing worse than a strained silence gradually filled with squawks and screeches to make the stranger feel uncomfortable.

> Allan came to church the first time because his wife had nagged him so much. He had every intention of saying to her, 'I've been, done it, and never again!' He went the next week though because he had enjoyed the singing so much. He went on to a nurture course, confirmation and leading and preaching.

Let's also recognize that people learn a lot of theology (good and bad) through the words of the songs and hymns. It is therefore important to choose them carefully. Graham Kendrick is known to have said, 'After all, a member of the congregation is far more likely to walk home humming the tune of one of the hymns (and thereby remembering the words) than reciting the main points of the day's sermon.'

> One very good practice is for you to go to another church for a change. Go and view it as an outsider and reflect on what is good and bad and allow that to inform you about your own church. It might be a good idea to let your minister know you are doing it and not all go on the same week!

Session 3: A welcoming God

If your church is short of musicians, or they have not reached their full potential, you may consider paying for one or two members to have music lessons and buying them some instruments. Some churches have always invested in a paid organist – also consider this option for gaining excellence by paying a worship-band leader. A good choir and good musicians of whatever style can lift the worship of the whole church but please don't announce 'a time of worship' when you actually mean singing! We worship God with our whole lives, not just when we sing to him.

Genuine warmth

Cold formality will not attract many people into the arms of the living God. Warm worship facilitates an authentic encounter between the church community and the living, loving God. It allows everyone to get caught up into the action for all are welcomed and involved. Warm worship helps newcomers see that this is the team they want to play for.

So the question is this – how can we make our worship warm and genuine? This is not just a question for the vicar or the worship leader or the choir master. It is for all of us because the spiritual temperature of the event is mainly controlled by the spiritual temperature of our own hearts. How can I best allow the warmth of my own relationship with God to shine through my worship? This is about how I sing, how I pray, how I respond to the preacher's joke, how I relate to people before the service, during the Peace and at the end. But it is also about how my relationship with God is nourished and sustained during the week. If I am used to praying and reading the Bible, and if I arrive a little early in order to prepare myself, then it is much more likely I will be one of the spiritual radiators in the church rather than one of the fridges.

Here is an old prayer: 'Lord renew your church and begin with me.' How can your own worship and relationship with God be renewed?

Accessibility

Some people respond spiritually to a cultivated sense of awe, wonder and mystery. But that is not the same thing as being unclear about what is going on and confusing people. Most people will respond better if they know roughly what is happening and why, if the language used in the notices, stage directions and sermon is straightforward, if the music culture is one that they resonate with, and if the prayers are couched in everyday language rather than in-crowd holy-speak. In fact any references or in-jokes that might leave newcomers feeling excluded or baffled should be kept to a minimum.

Gospel-richness

Christian worship is our loving response to all that God has done for us through Christ. Therefore, worship should tell the story of God's grace which stretches into the past and the future. It should also facilitate our response to God's grace. In addition, following Jesus requires a radical reorientation of our lives: e.g. taking on kingdom values, walking the way of the cross and living as slaves of Christ. Vibrant worship sensitively communicates the invitation to follow Christ.

Well-chosen hymns, songs and prayers, the use of images, candles, banners and film clips, well-prepared sermons and helpful rituals all have a part to play in telling God's story of grace to the community and inviting the community's response. They will also provide opportunities for all those present (including visitors) to see where (and how) their own story fits within the bigger story of God's people.

Some Christians think that we should go easy on 'Jesus' language with newcomers in case it puts them off. Usually it is Jesus who attracts and the church that puts people off. So do not be afraid of gospel-rich worship. Take people to the gate of heaven and they are likely to return for more.

Connecting with culture

Have you ever left a worship event feeling that you weren't allowed to be 'yourself' or that the worship made little or no connection with the world you know?

It is important for a community to see that worship is sparking within their contemporary world, in the midst of the life and culture they know. It is important in worship that we are all encouraged to bring the world to God and God to the world. Such an approach ought not be seen as a watering down of all that is 'holy' in church but a way of seeing God at work in all things – places, circumstances and resources. This then means that people feel able to bring their own lives (corporate as well as individual struggles, problems, thoughts, hopes and dreams) to church instead of feeling that they have to leave them at the door and collect them afterwards. This approach also means that we can communicate something of God, and worship him using creative resources available in contemporary culture (e.g. news, film, music and art) by weaving these into our worship. Those who are new may then be more able to make connections and find the familiar in an unfamiliar environment.

As our society is now multicultural in all sorts of dimensions (e.g. music) then we need a wide variety of worship cultures to connect with the wide variety of people living in our local areas. A robed choir and a Prayer Book service will be culturally appropriate to some people and in some contexts. An informal service with contemporary music and language will be culturally relevant for others. Neither worshipping community should belittle the other – both may be equally valid expressions of accessible worship for the people who attend them. But, of course, our key question is whether any particular act of worship is accessible to those people who might begin to attend it.

Some churches try to offer variety by making the service traditional one week and contemporary the next. This is usually a mistake. Not only do the regulars soon divide off into those who go '1st and 3rd Sundays' and those who turn up for the '2nd and 4th', but also newcomers can be put off the second or third time they arrive for worship as it is radically different from the event that attracted them first time around. Each worship event should be at the same time in the same place 52 weeks a year in roughly the same culture. Cultural diversity is best catered for by a variety of services not by wide variety within one.

Can you think of one way in which your church's worship could become more relevant to the everyday life of your neighbours?

Session 3: A welcoming God

Deepening relationships

Is anyone else tired of staring at the back of someone else's neck in worship every week, or is it just me? We convince ourselves that our worship events build community but do they really? Just because we stand or sit in rows, sing or speak together in the same place at the same time, does that build community? After all, genuine community requires authentic relationships, so how well do our worship events encourage and enable deeper relationships? More imagination is needed if this is to be worked out. This issue needs considering if we are to be truly welcoming. How could this be done in the context you are in? Interactive sermons may be one idea. Or how about asking the congregation to brainstorm some ideas, or set up a selection of interactive worship stations? But of course as far as newcomers are concerned such an approach may also be off-putting, so it may be a question of going gently and simply providing the opportunity in worship for people to say 'hello' to someone they don't know. Seeing the 'post-match' drinks as an essential part of the worship event may also be key. But of course, not everyone in church is comfortable chatting enthusiastically with strangers – some of us need a pillar to hide behind.

What practical things could be done to ensure that your worship helps the community to deepen relationships?

> **Almost immediately after the service the church warden went over to one of the visitors and sat next to him. Within a few seconds they were laughing together and chatting freely. The visitor informed him that his warmth towards him was really appreciated. He now attends each week.**

The traditional understanding of what we call 'services' is our service to the God who serves us. The traditional understanding of what we call 'liturgy' is a public work performed by the people for the benefit of others. Much of every worship event is not merely 'spoken liturgy' but 'animated liturgy' – serving God and others. How we go about things in worship demonstrates who we are and what we believe to newcomers and visitors. As Christians we of course want to demonstrate the grace of God. However, if I had a pound for every time I've seen musicians play and sing, or people welcoming at the church door, as if they really don't want to be there, I'd be rich. Of course we don't want to pretend about how we feel but it is crucial to remember that the way we go about things is just as important as what we do and the words we say in worship. This has implications for everyone and not just the 'up front' people. Generosity is a quality all of us can work towards – engaging fully in the worship, thanking people for their contribution, chatting with visitors or helping an elderly member of the congregation come forward to receive communion, to name but a few ways.

Doing things well with a generous spirit is therefore very important. People pick these things up. Worshippers will tell if we'd rather be reading the Sunday papers with a big mug of coffee. They will also notice if things are ill-conceived and ill-prepared. A friend of mine once said that the Holy Trinity is not honoured by the slapdash. Rublev's famous icon shows a generous welcome for all at the table of the Trinity. It seems natural then that the Trinity is honoured by our generosity towards others; in fact we participate with the Father, Son and Holy Spirit when we show generosity to others. Showing this through the time and effort given in preparing, leading and facilitating worship is a crucial part of providing a warm and genuine welcome to worship.

What small acts of generosity might make a big difference to the attractiveness of your church service?

Trinitarian focus

Trinitarian worship is worshipping the Father, with and through the Son, inspired by the Holy Spirit.

This of course may seem pretty obvious. But often, ensuring that worship is thoroughly Trinitarian can be a priority way down the list as the challenges facing us when trying to communicate the doctrine of the Trinity are very real. Also, churches that are light on liturgical text place much of the weight of responsibility for ensuring that worship is Trinitarian onto the songs, hymns and the preaching. Many songs are Unitarian in content, focusing on only one person of the Trinity. Careful use of the songs would ensure a Trinitarian focus: e.g. the collection of songs during a whole service providing a Trinitarian balance. The same can be true of preaching. But through a whole sermon or collection of sermons we can attempt to provide a balance.

Thoroughly Trinitarian worship holds the power to inspire a community to a greater expectation in worship events. With a more holistic view of God, everyone present will have greater opportunity to recognize that the living God (Father, Son and Holy Spirit) is available to be met. And, as we have noted, the Trinity is a community in which all find a welcome.

Thoroughly Trinitarian worship also helps ensure that worship is not overly focused on our subjective responses. It helps communicate the nature and character of the Triune God, his story of saving grace, his loving purposes in and for the world and his invitation to us to follow and serve. Faced with a fuller understanding of God, newcomers as well as old hands will be more able to respond to him in worship.

All involved

What's your learning style? How do you engage with the world? For example, are you a visual learner (preferring images, graphs and diagrams), a verbal learner (preferring to hear or read information), or are you someone who likes to learn by doing (an active or kinaesthetic learner)? In any community there is considerable difference and variation in learning styles among the people. And yet, almost invariably church worship favours those with a verbal learning style providing texts to read, speak, hear or sing.

Perhaps then it is time to redress the balance a little and, armed with our spirit of generosity, help more people engage in worship more easily. This may involve re-imagining our worship spaces by thinking of ways to communicate visually (through artwork, banners, candles or film). For those who are active learners, practical worship stations or rituals may be effective. For those who prefer to think things through, time for quiet reflection may be helpful.

In worship all should have the opportunity to be active team players and not simply spectators. This way we will dispel the consumer myth that worship is provided 'for me' by a few people. Transforming the 'audience'/'concert' culture of church to a 'hands on', 'participative' worship environment may help us provide a warm and genuine welcome to worship where all become valued and involved.

What sort of involvement works well in your church?

Creativity

For many, creativity is freedom, for others it feels like chaos. What is needed perhaps is a healthy framework for our freedom, to provide a strong foundation and structure for any creativity. The Church of England's worship resource *Common Worship* provides the rich inheritance of the past and contemporary frameworks with which to build creative worship. It encourages an 'imaginative engagement in worship, opening the way for people in the varied circumstances of their lives to experience the love of God in Jesus Christ in the life and power of the Holy Spirit' (*Common Worship* preface). Whatever service plan we choose to adopt (e.g. 'text light' Service of the Word or 'text rich' Order One Holy Communion) they provide the framework with which to build creative, imaginative worship that engages a diverse community. Common Worship in its very nature encourages us to remix the traditional, blend old and new. Tried and tested traditional resources and well-thought-out new ideas can work so well together. In fact, each can help unpack the meaning of the other.

The church has a wealth of worship resources at its disposal and yet so often we use the same few from a certain corner of church subculture. Instead of replicating the worship styles promoted by certain branches of the church (just as churches used to copy the cathedral model), churches might do better by serving fresh locally grown worship which newcomers may find more appetizing.

Can you think of something creative that might appeal to a newcomer?

3 Welcoming the children

The welcome and hospitality offered to children is a touchstone of any church's discipleship. It helps determine how close to the kingdom of God a church's life can get:

> **People were bringing little children to Jesus to have him touch them, but the disciples rebuked them. When Jesus saw this he was indignant. He said to them, 'Let the little children come to me, and do not hinder them, for the kingdom of God belongs to such as these. I tell you the truth, anyone who will not receive the kingdom of God like a little child will never enter it.' And he took the children in his arms, put his hands on them and blessed them.**
>
> **(Mark 10.13-16)**

A church welcomes children by helping them feel relaxed and at home and by giving them a really fun time. But most profoundly it welcomes children by enabling them to meet Jesus Christ their Saviour, treating them as fellow disciples and encouraging them to grow up all the way into Christian adults.

Inviting, welcoming, retaining, nurturing and discipling children in the Christian Church and faith is not just a job for specialists – it is the responsibility of the whole

Engaging all ages in worship

church community. The Church is always one generation away from extinction. Our main responsibility is to offer to God new adults who will be the Christian witnesses and leaders for the next generations.

The principal failure of the Church in recent decades has been our failure to invite, welcome, integrate, nurture and disciple the children. This is also the principal threat to the existence of churches in the future – most adult Christians have a church background as children. How can we attract as adults generations who have known nothing of church all their lives? A church composed increasingly of elderly people is a church that has abandoned the children or else the children have abandoned it. Absence of children is also the principal blight on the happiness of churches today – churches with no children or young people can be unhappy remnants, in mourning for a lost future.

Children's and youth work has clearly become harder for churches in recent years. Many churches have lost their role-model young adults who in the past helped lead and energize the children's work. Other adults – such as schoolteachers – have become more busy and exhausted in their employed lives and so have less time and energy to give to their natural church ministry. Children and young people themselves have much busier lives, especially on Sundays. The demands of the child protection legislation have discouraged many churches. When numbers fall below a critical level, the few remaining children no longer have a peer group to meet up with and so they lose their relational glue.

But the fact that we have to work harder to achieve results does not mean we give up. One vicar told me – 'We don't cater for teenagers in this church because we don't have any.' What comes first, the chicken or the egg? If our church stopped catering for adults, then before long we would have no adults either!

One good way of discovering the priorities of churches is to look at their budgets. Jesus said, 'Let the children come to me, do not hinder them.' Yet the majority of churches have a bigger budget for church flowers than for the whole children's and youth ministry. How would we defend that at the Day of Judgement?

But it does not have to be like that! Some churches still come alive with the laughter of children and the energy of teenagers. Other churches, bereft of children for years, are learning to include them again. In some dioceses we have learned to invest in children and young people, and there are once again increasing numbers in the churches. As with adults, the key is how the existing church members welcome the children and invest their time, love, expertise, prayer and money in them. And if lots more children start coming along then the church will never be the same again. So what is our priority – keeping the style of church and worship we are comfortable with, or sharing the love of the Lord Jesus Christ with the children?

Here is a set of options for how churches today can invite, welcome and integrate children and teenagers into their life. In some churches it may be appropriate to have these notes copied round the course members not only for general stimulation but also as the basis for an extra course session to consider how to improve your hospitality and facilities for the coming generations. The Members' Manual includes the following suggestion:

Over to you ...

If this may apply to your church then sound out other church members and leaders about meeting to plan a new and better era for the children and young people.

Inviting

Inviting children directly

Schools

Clergy contacts; the church team that goes into schools; the paid school-church worker; school events in church.

Clubs and festivals

Easter or summer holiday club; Activity Days; Christmas and other festivals.

Existing children

Encourage them to invite their friends. Put on social events and parties (e.g. the pancake party); have an annual Recruiting Competition with points and prizes for attendance and for bringing a friend; use 'Back to Church Sunday'.

Inviting their parents and families

A Marketing

Promoting the family or all-age service or the children's groups. Take leaflets etc. round the parish or the school; web site and notice board or your church DVD.

B Invitation

Asking existing parents to invite their friends or bring their children's friends; grandparents and other carers; 'Back to Church Sunday'.

C The church's programme

Invite members of the parent and toddler group, after school club, marriage and baptism contacts, and befriend those attending to get into the church school.

D Service time and style

Getting the timing right – teatime is a new good time. What about a Saturday or a weekday at the end of the school day? Work out the length and type of service that will encourage people to give it a try.

Welcoming

A The buildings

Easy to find and to park a car; safe and attractive pathway into the building; somewhere for buggies; happy bags with toys and quiet activities for small children to be given as they come into church; changing facilities; good quality toilets designed for children; space to move around (not boxed in by a pew); professional-standard kitchen; good quality and healthy food and drink; high-quality rooms and equipment for groups; play space at the end; specific attractions that make it a good experience for the child.

B The people

Warm welcome on entry – help to seats; explanation of how things work; smiles and fun; tolerance of children's behaviour patterns; existing families highly visible.

C The event

A good experience for parents and children – deep but interesting, allowance for short attention span; involvement of children while they are in the main worship event; Peace and communion well handled; chance to meet with God. Timing and style well thought through. Weekday options such as 'Messy church' considered (see **www.messychurch.co.uk**).

D The follow up

Contact details. Visiting. Explaining the system. Befriending.

Retaining

A Sustained quality

Not just the specials but every week needs to be a reasonable quality event. Spiritual nurture and encounter with God to be felt by children and parents.

B Progression

Keep trying new things – children get bored and feel they grow out of repetitive things. The next group up should always seem better and more interesting than the one a child is currently in. Make them ambitious to progress to the next group or stage.

C Priority for resources

Children's work has to be well resourced – rooms, equipment, training; trips and events; musical instruments etc.

D A place of safety

Child protection policies adhered to. No health and safety issues. Safe people in a safe environment.

E Integration

The children's ministry should be integral to the whole of church life, not a separate compartment or add-on. All adults should go out of their way to make the children feel happy and at home.

F Youth provision

Without it the children know they are expected to leave at 11. Children need older 'young people' as role models. Youth fellowship as the exciting group to aspire to. Many churches today do not have the leadership or the numbers of young people to form a viable youth group on their own. Churches have to work together – joint groups on the programme of all.

G Finding, training and keeping leaders

Always the key. Some of the best people should do this ministry. Consider paying a professional children's or families' or youth worker. Their role will be to recruit and train the team, take on the child protection issues, facilitate behind the scenes as well as be a mentor for the children.

4 Caring for people after the service

The few minutes after the end of the service can be the most testing and crucial of all for a newcomer or visitor or fringe church member. During the service you can relax because nothing much is expected of you. But now there is the possibility of people coming up to talk to you, or, worse, of being ignored. Most people who try out a church and are not talked to at the end of the service will not come again. At the very most they will give it one more try.

Sometimes nobody speaks to the newcomer because the church is not organized and no individual thinks it is their responsibility. If nothing else comes of this course in your church it will have been worthwhile if everyone now recognizes it is their own responsibility to welcome and be hospitable to newcomers. That probably needs to be said and agreed at a church meeting so that everyone knows it is their responsibility to talk to strangers.

But also, in all but the smallest churches, it is important to have a specialist 'Welcome Team' with a particular remit for encouraging those appearing on the edge of church life to come into the centre of its community and ministry. We suggest a 'belt and braces' approach – hospitality and welcome are the responsibility of all but also the special responsibility of the Welcome Team. The Welcome Team are not necessarily the people to do all the initial befriending but their role is to keep an eye on new people, introduce them to folk they might get on well with, make sure they are followed up, and encourage them through one or more of the routes into belonging we'll be dealing with in Session 4. The work of the Welcome Team starts with meeting newcomers at church services or other church events, but it does not stop there.

The final session of this course is designed as an initial training session for a Welcome Team. If one already exists we think the session will still be valuable because our concept of welcome accompanies newcomers much deeper in on their journey into belonging and contributing to the church than has been normal. If one does not already exist then we are encouraging you to think who to invite onto the Team and to start planning Session 5 of this course.

We are grateful to the Revd Tim Lomax for his invaluable contribution of insight, material and ideas relating to worship in this section.

Session 3: A welcoming God

Session 3 checklists

Session 3: A welcoming God and his welcoming people					
1 The initial welcome					
Do sidespersons/welcomers	**Yes/Good** 3 points	**OK/ Satisfactory** 2 points	**Could be better** 1 point	**No/Poor** 0 points	**Total points**
1 … welcome people outside or by the initial door?					
2 … appear smiling and confident?					
3 … have good identification – are easily found?					
4 … have a reasonably small bundle to pass over?					
5 … ever escort people to seats?					
6 … introduce new people to regular members?					
7 … adjust to the mood of different people arriving?					
8 … give you a warm welcome when you arrive?					
9 … know the congregation well enough to know who to pass newcomers on to?					
10 … represent all ages and types of people there at that service?					
Your Score out of 30 =					

An average score of 20 or more suggests your church is doing pretty well in this area. Under 20, and you might want to revisit your answers to see where improvements might be made in this general area. Any individual item scoring 1 or 0 may also need highlighting for improvement.

Is there a quick and easy way of improving your initial welcome you could try *next week*?

Session 3: A welcoming God and his welcoming people

2 The worship event

Questions	Yes/Good 3 points	OK/ Satisfactory 2 points	Could be better 1 point	No/Poor 0 points	Total points
1 Does your church service make you feel spiritually alive as you encounter God together?					
2 Is your worship easy for strangers to join in with and understand?					
3 Would newcomers always be shown the relevance of Jesus to their lives?					
4 Does your service help you to cope with the real world rather than being remote from it?					
5 Can you normally follow a clear overall theme to your church service?					
6 Are church members helpful towards strangers in worship?					
7 Does your church service place equal emphasis on God the Father, God the Son and God the Holy Spirit?					
8 Can everyone feel involved as participants not spectators?					
9 If an artist, actor, poet or jazz singer joined your church would they be able to contribute their talents to worship?					
10 Does your service come over as the best that this united group of Christians can offer to God? If you brought your next door neighbour to a church service what aspect of it do you think would most attract them and most repel them?					
Your Score out of 30 =					

An average score of 20 and above for this whole area suggests your church is doing pretty well in this area. Under 20, you might want to revisit your answers to see where improvements might be made in general. Any individual item scoring 1 or 0 may need highlighting for improvement.

Session 3: A welcoming God

Session 3: A welcoming God and his welcoming people

3 Welcoming the children

Questions	Yes/Good 3 points	OK/ Satisfactory 2 points	Could be better 1 point	No/Poor 0 points	Total points
1 Do you have good links with schools? (assemblies, church visits, school carol service etc.)					
2 Does your church put on holiday clubs for children?					
3 Are the church children encouraged to bring their friends?					
4 Are your family services and children's groups advertised widely in the area?					
5 Is there a good culture of inviting parents to bring their children?					
6 Is your service time a good one for local children?					
7 Are the buildings safe and attractive for children?					
8 Are the adults friendly to and tolerant of children?					
9 Do your service and groups nurture children spiritually?					
10 Is the quality of experience offered to children maintained well each week?					
11 Do you have a strong and committed children's team?					
12 Is there an adequate budget for children's work in your church?					
13 Is there a youth ministry for children to move on to?					
Your Score out of 39 =					

An average score of 26 or more suggests your church is doing pretty well in this area. Under 26, and you might want to revisit your answers to see where improvements might be made in this general area. Any individual item scoring 1 or 0 may also need highlighting for improvement.

What are your strong and weak points as a church and what do you think can be done about them?

Session 3: A welcoming God and his welcoming people

4 Caring for people after the service

Questions	Yes/Good 3 points	OK/ Satisfactory 2 points	Could be better 1 point	No/Poor 0 points	Total points
1 During the service is everyone invited to stay for refreshments?					
2 Do newcomers and fringe folk normally get chatted to by nearby regulars when the service ends?					
3 Are newcomers usually brought to the refreshments, not left to fend for themselves?					
4 Are there any church members with a specific responsibility to look after newcomers?					
5 Do the regulars seek out strangers to talk to rather than stick with their friends?					
6 Are the clergy free enough of other distractions after the service so they can meet newcomers?					
7 Is it normal to find out names and contacts on the first visit?					
8 Might an interested newcomer be given details of the church's life and be invited to other events?					
9 Might a newcomer receive a personal invitation to other events from a regular member?					
10 Is the general atmosphere happy and relaxed?					
Your Score out of 30 =					

An average score of 20 or more suggests your church is doing pretty well in this area. Under 20, and you might want to revisit your answers to see where improvements might be made in this general area. Any individual item scoring 1 or 0 may also need highlighting for improvement.

What can you do to make newcomers, visitors or people on the fringe feel at home at the end of church services?

Session 3: A welcoming God

Belonging

to the church community

■ Contents ■

■ Session 4 aim ■

The aim of this session is to enable the church to help newcomers who have begun attending church to start belonging to the church community. It will review key areas of church life where this belonging can take place in order to identify changes needed to encourage newcomers to fully integrate into the life of the church.

■ Session 4 outline ■

Welcome Housekeeping notices and prayer ....3 minutes

DVD Introduction Belonging: the glue that helps people to stick
and **People talking: What makes you feel you belong**? ....4 minutes

Word on welcome Reading: Ephesians 2.19 and Romans 12.5 with
brief comment ....5 minutes

Interview with two course members ....5 minutes

DVD Top tips for making people feel welcome in church ....6 minutes

Community life What goes on at our church? Compiling a list of the
social events in the church's programme ....5 minutes

Nurture and pastoral care Discussion of four case studies with reference
to nurture and pastoral care ....10 minutes

DVD Relationships Interview with Sara Savage...7 minutes

Christian service Discussion: does giving them a job keep them or drive
them away? ....5 minutes

Checklists Fill in all five checklists, discuss in pairs or groups then hand in.........20 minutes

So what did we learn? Sharing ideas and conclusions, announcing
checklist results ....15 minutes

DVD Authors' conclusion ....2 minutes

Course Prayer ....2 minutes

■ Session 4 leaders' notes ■

Getting the feel of it

Here are a couple of ideas for preparatory small group work:

1 Choose 4 scenarios (or use the ones in the course). In groups, role play with one person being the one with the need. Design a 'package' of help with the person. So often we give care which is not wanted and withhold what is. Always de-role after role play. Summarize what each scenario needed in the big group – would this actually happen in the church? What might enable it to?

2 Talk to a partner about 'If I could do any job in the church it would be …'. Make a list as a group of jobs, both those that exist and some that have been dreamt of.

3 Pairs work – 5 minutes each taking about a time when you needed extra care. What helped? What didn't? Share own experiences in the group.

Welcome Make sure everyone received a warm welcome and that checklists and pens are available. Remind them that this is the final session. Prayer.

DVD Introduction Belonging: The glue that helps people to stick and **People talking: What makes you feel you belong?** We focus on the nitty gritty of what causes people to make a lasting connection to a church. Church members talk about what made the difference for them.

Word on welcome Have someone read Ephesians 2.19 and Romans 12.5. Then comment on the readings along these lines:

> In these verses Paul talks about belonging. He uses various pictures, citizenship, family and body, and they all contribute to the idea of belonging. In this session we will be looking at how we can be a loving community that is warm and welcoming to new people God sends to us. To do this we will look at the five key areas of this session:
>
> **1** Personal friendship
>
> **2** Community life
>
> **3** Christian nurture
>
> **4** Pastoral care
>
> **5** Christian service

Refer back to the overall diagram of the course structure to remind course members of where Session 4 fits in.

Interview In the week prior to the session, ask two people to be interviewed and prepare them. Ask them to explain how they felt once they had begun coming to church; what helped them to feel fully part of the church and what nearly put them off. Aim for honesty, not simply being nice to each other.

Session 4: Belonging

DVD Top tips for making people feel welcome in church – a montage of our contributors who each give us their number one tip for making people feel welcomed in church.

Community life List as many different social events as possible on the flip chart, OHP or gizmo, firstly what the church does, then also what the church could do. At the end, emphasize the importance of personal invitation and of befriending new people while at the events, otherwise they are counter-productive.

Nurture and pastoral care Remind the members of the stories of the four case studies (page 84). Discuss how they would be nurtured and pastorally cared for in your church. What might you do to improve this? (If you have several groups you might wish to allocate them one study each or you may prefer to leave it to them to choose one.)

DVD Sara Savage will be talking about relationships, including how to read people – personality types – and how to be self-aware. How can we make people who aren't 'like us' still feel they can belong too?

Christian service 'It's no good getting 'em in if we don't keep 'em!' Does giving newcomers a job to do keep them or drive them away?

Checklists Fill in the five checklists and then hand them in to be collated and get five people to average out the scores for each of the five checklists.

So what did we learn? While the scores are being averaged out, invite each small group to give some feedback to the whole group – 'What is the most important thing we have uncovered during this session?'

Then announce the scores. Are there things either immediate or long term which need to be taken to the leadership of the church for recommended changes?

DVD Authors' conclusion A summary of the course and a challenge to take away.

Course Prayer Thank people for taking part. End with a prayer.

Time-saving tips In this session you may choose to interview only one person instead of two. Also, you could make a list of your church's social events on the flip chart or video projector and ask people to add any you have missed as well as suggestions for new ones.

Session 4 pre-reading

If you put this session into practice, you will not only help the newcomers, you will improve church life for everyone!

Below is an expanded version of the notes in the Members' Manual that we hope every course member will have read prior to Session 4. Please absorb the material below and have a look at the Members' Manual as well. Apart from helping you as a church leader, these notes might suggest something that is particularly appropriate to your church that you would like to communicate in Session 4.

Session 1 was about how to help people discover the church by making it more visible. Sessions 2 and 3 were about giving people a good initial experience of the church grounds and buildings, and of the church people. Now you come to the hardest part. How can newcomers who had a positive experience of attending your church event or service start belonging to your church community? There are five main routes into belonging:

1 Personal friendship

2 Community life

3 Christian nurture

4 Pastoral care

5 Christian service

Through opening up these routes we are trying to make a reality of the church ideal that Paul describes in his letters:

> **Consequently, you are no longer foreigners and aliens, but fellow citizens with God's people and members of God's household.**
>
> *(Ephesians 2.19)*
>
> **So in Christ we who are many form one body, and each member belongs to all the others.**
>
> *(Romans 12.5)*

We are not here looking at first contact and initial welcome but at what happens in the weeks and months that follow. When we think of the word 'church' we often think of 'worship' or 'preaching', but for most new people what's important is 'belonging' and 'togetherness'. Church growth experts, Bob and Mary Hopkins from Sheffield (**www.acpi.org.uk**), were once asked what they considered to be the most important factor in church growth. Their answer was, 'Glue! – whatever makes people stick.'

The nature of the glue may vary, but churches with good glue tend to grow. Sadly, in many churches, there is insufficient glue and people slip away, almost without being noticed. Imagine moving to a new area and attending a church for three or four weeks and then going missing to see what happened. Would anybody notice? What does happen after a few weeks when someone is no longer 'new' and not made a fuss of? This session is about developing a sense of belonging that enables faith to grow. It's about how to apply the glue that turns new attenders into members of the Body of Christ.

Session 4: Belonging

As you look at these materials keep in mind people you know who are new to church or use these four case studies to help to focus your thoughts:

Trish is a young single woman who has started to attend church. She has lots of problems and tends to tell people her troubles. At first they are attentive and caring, but after a few weeks she finds that people are avoiding her. After a while she stops coming – people notice but breathe a sigh of relief!

Andy and Gina had a new baby and enjoyed coming to church a few times. People played with the baby and were friendly to them. But no one wanted to be pushy so Andy and Gina hardly learned anyone's names and were never invited to anything else. When the baby began teething and they lost a lot of sleep they drifted away from coming and nobody seemed to mind. When they went to book the baptism for their second child they were nervous of what the vicar would say.

Flo is a recently bereaved widow. She has lost her self-confidence but used to go to church and now comes to find solace. She doesn't stay at the end of the service as she cannot face people. She's not sure what she's looking for and bit by bit finds other things to fill her time.

Stan has been coming to church for a few weeks. He's really enjoyed the services and is thinking of joining the course he's been invited to. He got the flu and was off work and missed church for two weeks. Then he had to visit family and so it's now three weeks since he's been. What will people think? What will they say? He's not sure of what the reaction will be so hesitates to come and misses a fourth week and a fifth ...

1 Personal friendship

Mrs Smith tried a church for the first time and, over coffee afterwards, a regular said to her, 'It's a very friendly church here.' Mrs Smith retorted: 'I don't want a friendly church. I want a church where I can make friends.'

For a newcomer, the fact that church members are friendly with each other is irrelevant; what counts is whether they are prepared to make friends with them. If someone makes a few friends in a church in the first few weeks they will stay, if not they won't.

Do newcomers find it easy to make friends in your church? Ask the newer people at church about their experience. Even better, ask someone who tried the church but didn't stick.

Improving your befriending skills

The first step is to find out a person's name. It makes a world of difference to greet someone by name when they come back next time. If you're forgetful, like me, you'll need help. When first introduced to someone, keep using their name in your conversation – that helps it to lodge in your memory. When you part company, jot the name down in your diary or a notebook. Just writing it down helps to keep it in your memory, and you can look it up to remind

Chris Acher shares his top tips for a welcoming church

yourself next week before they come. If they turn up and are greeted by you saying, 'Hello Fred, lovely to see you again!' it will really make them feel welcomed and help them belong. But if you lose the record and can't remember their name, be honest and ask them. Don't try to pretend that you know – you'll get caught out and that is worse than forgetting in the first place.

The next step is to find out their contact details. This is vital. If newcomers stop coming after two or three weeks (or six or seven) it may be for a very innocent reason like illness, but they invariably feel awkward about coming back. If you have no contact details you have not got very far in befriending them and growing their relational glue. Alternatively, if you want to invite them to something that is happening, you need their details. Remember, many younger people communicate by email or text so make sure you get their email address and mobile number! There is more than one way of contacting people these days.

How do you get their details? In conversation, perhaps over refreshments after a service, ask, 'Do you live round here?' People often give the road in which they live and then it is easy to say, 'What number?' If they ask why, be honest, it's so you can invite them to anything that is happening and if they are ill and go missing you can check that they are OK.

Or you may use a welcome card (see Document A on page 105 for an example). Some churches put these in the pews/chairs and expect people to fill them in. People rarely do this without being asked – and someone needs to ensure they are always replenished. Whether they're in the pews/chairs or at the back of the church, welcome cards make it easy, while chatting to someone, to suggest that they fill one in. You might offer to fill it in for them there and then.

> **One church has a welcome booklet and instead of giving this to newcomers while they are in the church they deliver it to them with a simple letter of welcome from the vicar (see Document B on page 106 for an example). So one approach is to say, 'Please give us your contact details and we will deliver you the booklet.' Simple. Easy. Calling round with a welcome pack/booklet is a good first step in friendship.**

Make sure you have one person who collates all the information about new people whether this is from a card or informal conversation. This is especially important if you have more than one main service and the new person tries them all out! If you have a Welcome Team it would make sense for it to be one of them.

Difficulties to watch out for

There are at least two main types of visitor you will be dealing with. The first type is a person new to the church, with little or no faith background. Some will prefer to remain anonymous since they want to retain control. Others may have come with the motive of finding friendship and community, and they will usually be pleased to open up about themselves. The second type is the Christian who has moved into the area or is looking for a new church. You can often tell if someone is familiar with church by how they handle themselves in the service (singing the hymns, finding their way easily in the books etc.). In most cases these will want to be known and have a fuss made of them. Such a person will generally not feel overwhelmed or put off by an early invitation to your house for supper or to your cell group meeting and new friendships can form very fast, whereas someone new to the church may find this too much, too soon.

Occasionally you might encounter someone who has been hurt in their last church and so wishes to remain anonymous. In such a situation, pick up the clues to back off. Rarely will someone tell you directly that they do not want to give information about themselves. They are more likely to make excuses about needing to get home or escaping to the toilet. If, when you ask a question, they close it down immediately, then take the hint and do not push them. Also, look for body language. If the person avoids eye contact or shies away, respect their privacy. Some people simply do not want to give their details. In such a case you must simply be friendly with them when you meet them, opening up about yourself and helping them to begin trusting you. They may open up about themselves when they are ready to.

If you are getting to know a newcomer but realize you are not going to be a natural friend for them, introduce them to other church members who may be. Perhaps they are at a similar life-stage, or live nearby, or have shared interests or sense of humour. Involve others in the business of offering friendship. If you invite the new people round to your house you might also invite a few other congregation members as well. If you invite the new chap to go to the football match with you, you may wish to take along another congregation member as well.

Friendship

The offer of friendship is simply that – it has no ulterior motive, simply a desire to welcome someone into a healthy community for their sake plus the pleasure you take in their company and in getting to know them. You might even find yourself 'entertaining angels unawares' (Hebrews 13.2). You do not need to talk about religion to begin with, but rather find your common interests and invite them to join you for

Sara Savage

everyday activities. If they are new to the area, offer to show them round. Most people today start to belong to a church before they begin to believe its message. Your job in offering friendship is simply to help them belong. If religious conversation comes around, that is fine, but there is no need to force it.

One of the first steps in belonging to the Body of Christ is to make friendships with other believers. The circles of friendships in churches are often very close. Are we prepared to open up our circle to include new people? This is the challenge of hospitality – making room for the new person. It will mean change and is costly, but in the end it is one of the most enriching aspects of church life.

2 Community life

> The Harvest Supper was in full swing with ripples of laughter floating through the hall. I was really nervous about coming but I'm so glad I accepted Fred's invitation – and the free ticket. Some of the turns left a bit to be desired but no one seemed to mind that Peggy sang out of tune and Jack forgot his lines in the middle of that dreadful monologue. It was all such fun and when Joe on our table won the raffle he shared the chocolates with all of us! I haven't laughed as much in ages. I've met so many people and learnt who different people in the church are. Even the vicar has a sense of humour! Going to church will never be the same after this – I'll feel part of them.

Most churches have active social programmes through which new members can become part of the family of the church. It's something many churches are really good at and need to make the most of. Have you noticed how often new people come along to the social events?

Over to you ...

List your church's social events. How suited are they to newcomers? What other events could you try?

There is no end to the list of possibilities for social events and each church is unique, but here are just a few of the things that happen:

Informal bring and share meal. Picnic. BBQ. Barn dance. Film evening. Community fun day. Cinema evening. Treasure hunt. Quiz night. Pub evening. Rambling (no, this is not a reference to the sermon!).

> We moved to a new village and someone said, sniffily, to one of our new friends, 'I hope they'll come to the community centre social.' Our friend said, 'Have you invited them?' 'Oh no!' came the answer. Even though we saw a poster advertising it we didn't feel we could gatecrash uninvited so of course we didn't go!

Social events can be seen to be for the 'regulars' so do make sure they are publicized and newcomers are invited otherwise they will actually feel excluded by them. It's no good having lots of things happening if new people know nothing about them. If you are having a social event put up posters so everyone who comes to church, even for the first time, is aware of what is happening. If you have a notice sheet, make sure the details go into it for everyone to see. It's no good trusting the grapevine to inform people of events – it will work for the regulars but not the new people. And if at these events the church regulars keep themselves to themselves and ignore the new people, they will be a point of exclusion, not inclusion.

Some churches hold specific events for newcomers. In one church the minister and his wife invited every new person in the church to come for an evening meal. It wasn't a small church so this was a huge commitment, but it worked for them with their gifts and style of leadership. In another church, every six months they held a Newcomers' Tea Party. Everyone who'd started coming to church in the last few months was invited on one Sunday afternoon where the church staff and key leaders introduced themselves, explained how the church works and then had a bun fight. Most people said how much they enjoyed it and how valuable they found it. Another church commented that the most useful thing they found was the new persons' cup of tea event with the pastoral team after the Sunday service which led to many settling in church. In each of these situations, new people could ask questions about the life of the church and start to develop friendships.

Does your church have a 'Welcome Leaflet' or 'Welcome Booklet' that lists everything that happens? It's good to give everyone a copy but be sure to add something like, 'You're welcome to everything but we don't arm twist you to anything.' Make sure you include how to join these activities and have a contact person (with phone number) for each one. They are not secret societies for the initiated – but they sometimes seem like this to the outsider. It may well be that everyone in the church knows all church meetings start at 7.30 p.m. but the newcomer doesn't! Also, if you have a welcome leaflet or booklet, make sure it is kept up to date so that newcomers don't turn up to something that stopped two years ago!

Some churches produce A5 fliers for each of their church activities so that the members can give one of these to a new person they think might be interested. That man who has come alone can be invited to the men's group – by the men! That young mum with the pram and baby can be invited to the toddlers' group – by the other mums. In both cases they have the flier to remind them and to give them all the information they need. It takes a bit of organizing but pays dividends. In fact the Welcome Booklet of some churches is made up of a collection of these A5 fliers in a neat folder – then that keeps all the information up to date.

Perhaps all this talk of leaflets and posters sounds to you like the out-of-date ramblings of soon to be pensioned-off clergy. For many churches and people, communication is better made through the church web site, the email list, the group text or the DVD. Instead of a church magazine to give to a newcomer, consider making a church DVD showing clips of your various services and events, and also interviews with church members about their faith-journey and church involvement. Or just give people the web address where they can hopefully find out all they need to know about your church. Offer your church not as an organization to belong to and find a job in but as a relational community that offers to accompany new people on their spiritual journeys. However, a church without posters, notice sheets and other publicly available invitations will feel even more like a closed club open only to those who have passed some sort of membership test. Perhaps we need to keep using paper as well as the modern electronic communication gizmos.

It is vital to invite new people to your event personally. Don't just depend on a poster, a slot in the notices or the electronic ether. Personal invitation that says 'Come with me' always works best. Some may say, 'I invite people but they never come.' Perhaps we all need to go out of our way and say, 'I'll call for you and go with you.' Above all, be friendly! Even if we put on all the right events if we don't befriend people through them they will not stick!

3 Christian nurture (growing in faith)

> **Evelyn walked up to the vicar with a beaming smile. She had just completed the new 'beginners' course' and wanted to tell him how good it was. 'I've learnt more about Christianity in the last ten weeks than in all those sermons in the last three years!' she announced. He didn't know whether to be pleased or not!**

We don't want people simply to attend church, we want them to come to faith in Christ and grow in faith – 'To grasp how wide and long and high and deep is the love of Christ' (Ephesians 3.18).

Over to you ...

Read Paul's prayers for the church in Ephesians 1.17,18 and 3.16-21 and make them your ambition for the people of your church both old and new.

But spiritual growth does not happen automatically. People tend to take several years coming to full Christian faith. We need plenty of opportunities to learn about the faith, ask our questions and make our response.

> Chris started attending church through meeting the curate's wife on an Open University course. We were rejoicing a few months later when she responded to a call in a service to commit her life to Christ. But when she gave her testimony a few years later, I was astounded that the date she gave for committing her life to follow Christ was 18 months after the date when we had all rejoiced!

In the past many people had a good grounding in the Bible and the Christian faith. This gave them a head start when they decided to be practising Christians. Today, many people know very little about Christianity, not even the basic Bible stories or the Lord's Prayer. We must provide more help and information to enable people to make their decision whether to follow Christ and to equip them to live the Christian life. This is where the nurture course, or Christian basics courses, such as Alpha, Emmaus and Start! come in.

Many churches have found nurture courses invaluable not only for helping people explore the faith but also for helping them grow key friendships. There is nothing new about these courses. We have been doing confirmation courses and membership courses for ages. Today, however, we have people who wish to explore the Christian faith but are not ready to make the commitment to the church that confirmation and other membership courses entail. Nurture courses provide a place to explore questions of faith without demanding commitment to the church.

There are courses to suit a whole range of different churches and church traditions. They have been packaged to provide excellent materials in an accessible way. Most of them give helpful advice on how to set up a nurture group and run the course.

Choosing a course

Find a course where the content suits your church. Some courses are more catholic in tone (Knowing God Better), some are conservative evangelical (Christianity Explored), some are broad church (Emmaus) and some are charismatic (Alpha). For further details please turn to page 93.

Make sure the style suits the people you are aiming at. Some are DVD-based with a talk that can be quite long (Alpha and Christianity Explored) – this works for some but not for others. Some are more interactive (Start!) while others are more experiential (Essence).

Decide what length of course is right for you. Some are put off by a ten-week course and prefer six weeks as being more manageable, while others think that ten weeks makes it more possible for the group to bond together. It might be that you are holding a special church event after which you will run a nurture course and if you run a ten-week one it will run into the holidays and therefore you need a shorter course.

Look carefully at initial and ongoing costs. Some of the courses have a high original cost for the package but then are relatively cheap since after the original payment all you need to do is photocopy the worksheets. Others have ongoing costs for booklets but then course members have these booklets for future reference. In the table on page 93 we have attempted to give an indication of the cost for running a course with 12 participants.

None of the courses is perfect and all have their drawbacks. Some people decide to write their own, or mix them together, or run one after another. You have to decide what is right for you but do make the most of the excellent quality resources available. Most of the courses have web sites from which you can find out more details.

Setting up a nurture course

So, having looked at all the courses and decided which one you think will suit you, how do you go about setting up a nurture course? Here are some of the basic questions you need to consider.

Think carefully about where to hold the course. Some prefer to use the church buildings as participants then identify with the church and this hopefully makes the next step into church easier. Others prefer a non-church, more neutral venue so people are not put off by it being too 'churchy'. It can be possible to use homes but many people are becoming increasingly wary of inviting strangers into their homes, and it can make providing a meal difficult. However, where you can use a home, perhaps your own, this may be the best venue for relaxing people and developing good relationships. Many tend to use a church building or church rooms but if you decide on this option, make sure everything is arranged for maximum comfort, warmth and welcome. It's no good having six people feeling lost in a cavernous church hall or 26 people crammed into a tiny back room. Aim at creating the right setting where the chairs are arranged comfortably, the leader can see everyone (and everyone can see the screen if there is a DVD), and there is good light and ventilation.

When will you hold the course? Will it be in the daytime or the evening? Some people are only available in the evenings, whereas others (elderly people) would never come out at night, especially when the evenings are drawing in. Some churches alternate between a daytime nurture course and an evening one – some churches run both at once.

Then look at when you want the course to start. It may follow a major outreach event or mission, or may be after 'Back to Church Sunday'. Then look at when the course will end. It would be difficult to start a ten-week course a few weeks before the summer holidays as many would miss parts of the course because of going away. Some people also prefer the course to end before Christmas or Easter but others quite like the idea

Session 4: Belonging

of a couple of sessions after the holiday so that they can gather people together again for the end of the course and then hopefully direct them into something else.

Have the publicity ready well in advance. Some courses have ready-made publicity. If not, produce some yourself that can be handed out by congregation members to invite people – a simple leaflet is easy to produce. It's no good expecting people to invite their friends and neighbours if they have not been given the time and the means for doing so.

Most people will join a course not as a result of publicity but through personal invitation. By all means encourage every congregation member to invite someone onto the course but also compile a list of warm contacts or newcomers or people on the fringe of church life you think might benefit from the course. If you have a Welcome Team this could be a job for them.

Decide if you are going to include a meal with the course, or not. Some courses highly recommend this and see it as part of the whole process. Be aware of the extra workload this may create. Some churches have stopped running nurture courses because they can't get anyone to do the meals! If it's a choice between running a course without a meal or not running one at all, find a different way of doing the 'social' bit.

One church in Blackpool was in an area where everyone had their tea at teatime. Doing an evening meal as part of the nurture course just wouldn't work. So they started the meeting with a cuppa and an assortment of really nice cream cakes. It fulfilled the same social effect as the meal for a fraction of the cost and effort, was very successful and was culturally relevant!

Whatever you decide, make sure you don't stint on quality.

It's good to have a few helpers on the course to build friendships with those who come. If you have a large number of candidates, the helpers can be used to lead the discussion in small groups. Choose people who will be sensitive to the outsider. You do not want someone who will dominate the discussion or preach at people.

The Achilles heel of most nurture courses is what happens afterwards. Too often course members are simply expected to attend church services and no other guidance or provision is made. Alternatively, sometimes course members are bludgeoned to attend something else and feel pressurized. Each course participant should be given an opportunity to discuss their own personal next step. It is important to have something for those who wish to explore Christianity further. Some churches have a range of midweek fellowship groups or cell groups to offer to those who have completed the course. Other churches run a follow-on course, either another nurture course that complements the first one, or a course that looks at developing areas of faith. This can then, in time, become an ongoing fellowship or cell group. Some may want to do the course again, and often gain more from doing it a second time, but beware of those who never move on. Some will have done enough for the moment and it is important to allow them the freedom to end their involvement at this stage.

Here are some of the commonly used courses for you to compare.

Course	Tradition/ style	Number of sessions	DVD	Meal	Weekend/ Awayday	Photocopiable worksheets	Minimum cost for 12 participants and 1 leader
Alpha	Evangelical charismatic	10	Yes	Yes	Yes	No	£160.00
Christianity Explained	Evangelical	6	No	No	No	Yes	£9.00
Christianity Explored	Conservative Evangelical	10	Yes	Yes	Yes	No	£94.00
Emmaus	Anglican	15	No	No	No	Yes	£22.50
Essence	Modern Spirituality	6	CD	No	No	N/A	Free download
Evangelium	Catholic	25	Yes	No	No	No	£120.40
Knowing God Better	Catholic	7	Yes	No	No	Yes	£34.90
Start!	Evangelical	6	Yes	No	No	Yes	£39.95

P.S. New courses are constantly being produced. The web site is being regularly updated with the latest information about nurture courses. Look at: **www.everybodywelcome.org.uk** for an up-to-date summary of available courses.

4 Pastoral care

> **Marie has been attending church for a few months. Since she came to the carol service and was clearly touched by God, she has hardly missed a week though her husband never came. Then someone noticed she was missing for three weeks. She hadn't made many friends in church yet and so I went to visit, unsure of what sort of reception I would get. Something had happened to a friend and she'd hit a crisis of faith and we were able to talk it through and pray. Next Sunday she returned and before long her husband started coming. If I hadn't done that visit ...**

There are many stories similar to Marie's but how many stories are there that we know nothing about because the person has slipped away unnoticed? Once we start to come to church this is only the beginning of our journey of faith. Far too many people fall away after the first few weeks, or the first few months. The Parable of the Sower (Matthew 13.1-9) makes it clear that some will slip away but this is not an excuse for poor pastoral care. It is not enough simply to put the name and number of your 'pastoral coordinator' on the weekly notice sheet – we need to be proactive in pastoral care: 'Be sure you know the condition of your flocks, give careful attention to your herds' (Proverbs 27.23).

It is often considered that it is the job of the minister to visit everyone, as well as all the other things he or she is expected to do! Gone are the days of the local parish church with one minister for 300 houses – if it ever existed. If effective pastoral care is to take place then it is everyone's responsibility. The very best pastoral care flows naturally from loving, caring relationships and you should never underestimate how much of this does happen in our churches. However, no congregation is perfect and people do get missed out. This is especially true of the newer people into church who have not fully become part of the church family.

Churches have tried all sorts of ways to improve their pastoral care. These are best considered as 'safety nets' to catch those who, for one reason or another, do not get picked up by the natural love and care of the congregation. In no way are they to be seen as replacing spontaneous love and care. Here are some of the different pastoral safety nets that churches have developed.

Pew pastors are appointed in some churches. We are all creatures of habit and most of us sit in the same place each week. Key people are selected who will keep an eye on a section of church and get to know the congregation seated in their area and when they notice someone missing get in touch with them. Of course, this is something that happens naturally but it can be helpful to ask certain individuals to see it as their way of serving. The danger in this is that it works for those who have been coming for years but those who have only been coming a few months and are not well known can still easily be missed – and if they are missed, often no one knows how to contact them.

Small groups are the answer for some churches. As many members as possible are encouraged to join home/small groups where the pastoral care can take place. Once in a small group someone should be befriended, prayed for and followed up if they go missing. This also applies to newcomers who are encouraged into a nurture group and after that, into a fellowship group. In the smaller group good relationships can be built and it is easy to see when people are missing and to know their circumstances. This is also very helpful where we see the habit of weekly church attendance evaporating and so people may only be attending on a Sunday once every two or three weeks. Some churches take a hard line and the congregation are told that unless they are in a small group they cannot expect any pastoral care; other churches take a softer line and presume those in a small group are catered for and then try to keep a closer eye on those not in small groups. These groups can include the Men's Fellowship, Mothers' Union, choir or cleaning team as well as Bible study groups. However, some small groups are better at pastoral care than others and it is dangerous to presume all small groups are good at their pastoral care. If small groups are used for pastoral care, it is vital to know who is in groups and who is not. However, in most cases no more than 50 per cent of church members are in small groups and so this leaves a huge percentage not cared for if all your eggs are in this pastoral basket.

Attendance registers are kept by some churches.

In one church in Blackpool the morning congregation grew and so two services were created. After a couple of months the vicar considered that people had settled into the service which suited them so took out the electoral roll and jotted down which service he thought each person was attending. When he checked the following Sunday his estimate was out by miles. He thought, 'If I don't even know which service people are attending, how on earth can we care for them pastorally?' He decided to take a register for a few weeks to see which service people were attending and found it so useful in spotting who was missing that he continued to do it and trained a pastoral team to help in this also. If someone went missing they would receive a phone call or visit to see if they were OK. It became invaluable as attendance patterns changed with some people only coming once every three or four weeks. It also meant that new people's names were learnt quickly. Most of the congregation thought it was great because someone noticed when they were missing and called to check if they were OK, but one or two objected. Document C on page 107 is a sample of a pastoral care register.

P.S. They did not call a register from the front – it was easy to complete the list from the back of the church so it was not intrusive.

Alphabetical grouping is used by some churches with a pastoral team who carve up the electoral roll between them on an alphabetical basis. They can each then decide on the appropriate level of pastoral care. The difficulty with this is that many new people are not on the electoral roll and so would be missed out by this system. It is possible to add their names to the list, though there is still the danger of missing out the most vulnerable who are the least well known.

In all of this it is important to coordinate pastoral care and welcome. In some churches the pastoral carers are also the key welcomers so there is no problem of them relating together. If a church has a Welcome Team (or person) separate from the pastoral team they need to work out together when someone stops being the responsibility of the welcomers and comes under the care of the pastoral team.

In general it is better if both are caring for them than if they both presume the other is, and no one does it!

Over to you ...

Refer back to the four case studies on page 84. How would they be nurtured and pastorally cared for in your church? How would you try to stop them (and others) leaving your church?

Remember never to take for granted the established members, even if they are in positions of service themselves. Who 'cares for the carers'? It is good when pastoral

Session 4: Belonging

carers or group leaders meet together, not only to show care and concern for others but to watch out for each other. These meetings are an opportunity for the church leadership to come alongside and show care for those who care for others.

5 Christian service

In most churches there is a small active group who do most of the work – church being like a passenger liner where a small crew work hard making life pleasant for all the passengers.

All Christians are called to serve others and use their gifts for the sake of the whole church. It is important for every congregation member, new and old, to develop and grow in Christian service. In this consumer society, how do we help people to be contributors who talk about 'our church' rather than 'this church'?

In our present culture, 'commitment' is a dirty word. People are reluctant to commit themselves to a weekly (or even monthly) activity. Lifestyles have changed over the last 25 years and now people are often away at weekends visiting relatives or going on weekend breaks. In the past there was an army of housewives who took up all types of voluntary roles but they are now either working or looking after the grandchildren (or great-grandchildren!). This has affected not only the church but many voluntary organizations as well.

As a result, many churches are struggling to find people to fill the roles needed to maintain the work. It is therefore very tempting when someone new arrives to think in terms of 'What can we get this person to do?'

> **The minister could hardly believe his ears. As he talked to the new woman who had just started attending his church with her two children, she explained that in the past she had been a Sunday school teacher. His smile widened when she mentioned that her husband, who would have been there but he had a bad cold, played the keyboard. He struggled to hide his delight when she explained that he was also an accountant – not only might they be good givers, but they needed a new treasurer, were short of Sunday school teachers and desperately needed help with the music. As he walked away he allowed the grin on his face to show and he was considering whether the first week she attended was too soon to ask her to get involved. Little did he know that her friend who had invited her had got her to come by saying how much they desperately needed help!**

There are two different ways of approaching this. One group says, 'Give 'em a job to do as soon as possible, then they feel part of everything. That's the best way to keep them!' The other says, 'Don't scare people off by instantly pouncing on them to do a job no one else is willing to do. Get to know them, let them grow in trust and spirituality before using them!' Well, those are two opposing philosophies. Both have points to commend them, and drawbacks.

Julia was asked to take charge of the reading rota. She had been in the church for quite a while and knew most people so she seemed ideal. The church didn't count on the fact that Julia had a heart for the outsider and she asked all the new people to do the readings. The long-standing church members were incensed – being asked to do a reading was a sign of being fully a member, not for newcomers. 'Exactly!' thought Julia.

Over to you ...

Does giving new people a job to do keep them or drive them away?

Christian service is not just, or even primarily, about having a job in the church. It is about living Christianly out in the world. For some people, belonging is not enhanced through taking a job in the church but by being supported by the church in their demanding lives outside it. Individuals vary. That is why it is good practice, when someone has been coming to church for a little while, for the minister or another designated leader to have a private discussion with them about how they would like to develop their membership and contribution.

Many churches begin with a list of jobs to fill and then see whom they can pick off to fill the gap. Unfortunately, it is not always the person most suited to the task. The danger of this approach either with a newcomer to the church or as a long-term strategy is that we begin with the point of need rather than looking at the gifts of the person. Look at a person's SHAPE – Spiritual gifts, Heart, Abilities, Personalities, Experiences. People are more likely to be fruitful and fulfilled if their 'shape' is taken into account rather than being shoved as a round peg into a square hole just because there is a need. This applies to their Christian living out in the world just as much as any jobs in the life of the church.

By and large, those in their twenties, thirties and forties are much less likely than older generations to accept a role that does not really fit their passion, energy and shape. People will be unhappy and may leave if the church tries to mould them into being church-shaped people, perpetuating hangovers from the past. They will be fulfilled and will stay if they themselves are helping mould a people-shaped church whose style and ministries arise from the energies, passions, gifting and shape of today's church members.

In some churches certain roles are seen as a reward for long service and the gifts and temperament of the person are not taken into account. In one church a lovely man was encouraged to train as a Reader as this was the only way to give him 'recognition' for his caring pastoral heart. But, he couldn't lead services for toffee and it was agony both for him and the congregation.

The difficulty most people have in volunteering to do something is that it may be a life sentence. We all know the story of someone who agreed to help out in Sunday school when there was a crisis and they are still doing it 25 years later. The problem now is that this has become their identity and their seat of power and they will not give it up, even though they don't like children! Of course, new people may not realize it's a life sentence – until it's too late!

Here are some helpful ground rules for tasks in church.

1 Have a clear job description. It need only be brief but many people take something on not really knowing what is expected of them. They can either feel a failure as they are not sure they are doing it right, or can be seen as a failure by others even though they have never had it explained to them. It can also help to make sure things are done correctly.

2 Have a probationary period and a time limit. It's good to have a built-in review. If it's not working after three months (or six if you prefer), it's best to look at this honestly, rather than have resentment building up which may lead to the person leaving the church. If a job is seen as being for three years after which it is quite acceptable to lay it down, you are much more likely to have people opting into it. It can always have an extension of a further three years.

3 Offer training. This applies whether it is the treasurer who needs guidance about church structures and practices, or the tea rota where people need to be shown where things are and how they work. If you can't provide it, find someone who can. Perhaps a group of churches or deanery might be able to do this together.

4 Give people responsibility, but with accountability. Don't leave them to sink or swim. It's important to allow people to be creative and make their mistakes but it's equally important to be aware of what is happening and give support and advice where needed.

5 Affirm people in their service. We all need to be encouraged rather than taken for granted. A gentle word of appreciation goes a long way.

6 Beware of stagnation. We tend to leave something alone if it's working OK. We need to keep reviewing activities and people so they do not stagnate. Sometimes areas of service need to change (or cease) and people need a new challenge to move forward in their Christian discipleship and service.

It's easy to talk about 'every-member ministry' but it's much harder to do it and to lead it. Often it's simpler to do the job ourselves rather than risk someone else (or someone new) doing it. The more people we have doing things, the more there is to 'manage' and many church leaders are not good 'managers' and don't want this role. It may be that an important point in the growth of the church is to acknowledge this and find a person or team who can manage and train others.

Another problem is that some of the less glamorous jobs struggle to get people involved. Why is it these days that no one seems to want to be involved in work with children? What more vital job can there be in a church apart from nurturing our children in the faith? Yet over and over again churches are struggling to get anyone at all to work with the children or those doing it would love to give it up but cannot because it would collapse. How can we encourage more people to serve in difficult areas?

Two key things in this whole area are teaching and vision. Consider doing a sermon series on service and gifts. There are some great biblical passages (1 Corinthians 12.7-11;

Romans 12.3-8; Ephesians 4.11-13; 1 Peter 4.7-11) on which to base this teaching on gifts but it also needs to be centred on the value of 'service' (Mark 10.41-5) rather than 'position'. We also need to raise people's vision of what they are doing. Do you remember the story of the man who visited St Paul's Cathedral when it was in its construction stage? He asked one worker what he was doing and he replied, 'I'm building a wall.' The second worker he asked responded, 'I'm earning money to feed my family.' The third answered, 'I'm helping Christopher Wren build a great cathedral to God's glory.' In church we're building a community of faith to glorify God and to share his love with others. Let's invite people into this exciting venture and not lose sight of it ourselves!

There are various exercises that can help us to look at our gifts and where we use them. Here are samples but there are many others:

- *Play your Part*, by Sally Beyer (Windmills, University of Liverpool)
  http://gartreemp.blogspot.com/2008/06/play-your-part.html
- *Life Calling*, by Robert Warren and Kate Bruce (Church House Publishing)
- Network Course, by Willow Creek. There have been various adaptations of these materials **http://www.willowcreek.org.uk/resource.php?r=10**

The worst thing you can do is embark upon one of these and then not follow it up – people will have offered themselves to serve and then not had it taken up. Make sure that whatever you begin is manageable and achievable.

An excellent place for the development and nurture of gifts is the small group. Here is a place where people can exercise all sorts of gifts as well as develop a sense of belonging and forge sound relationships.

Conclusions: keeping growing

We never reach the point where we are fully mature and do not need to develop further. Sadly, some people fade away from the church after several years because there is no further challenge in discipleship or service. Everyone needs to keep growing and be challenged.

Small groups are very important but watch out for stagnation. Some groups or individuals need to change to grow further.

Pastoral care needs to be maintained for everyone but with a special eye being kept on those who are relatively new.

It is vital to keep under review where people are serving and see what new opportunities there are.

And remember, people today do not want to be part of an institution but they are desperate to be part of a family! Remember – glue!

Session 4 checklists

Session 4: Belonging
to the church community

1 Personal friendship

Questions	Yes/Good 3 points	OK/ Satisfactory 2 points	Could be better 1 point	No/Poor 0 points	Total points
1 Do you have some good friends at your church?					
2 When you joined your church did you make friends quickly and easily?					
3 Do you have a good system for getting contact details from newcomers?					
4 Are there people in your church with the time and energy to make friends?					
5 Do you have a wide variety of people in your church so that most newcomers would find a natural friend?					
6 As far as you know, do newcomers get contacted quickly?					
7 Do congregation members go out of their way to befriend newcomers?					
8 Have you become friendly with new people who have joined your church in the last year?					
Your Score out of 24 =					

An average score of 16 or more suggests your church is doing pretty well in this area. Under 16, and you might want to revisit your answers to see where improvements might be made in this general area. Any individual item scoring 1 or 0 may also need highlighting for improvement.

Is your church a 'friendly church' or a place where people can 'make friends'? Are there any changes that need to be made?

Session 4: Belonging
to the church community

2 Community life

Questions	Yes/Good 3 points	OK/ Satisfactory 2 points	Could be better 1 point	No/Poor 0 points	Total points
1 Does your church have a social life that is really good with a regular round of social events suited to most congregation members?					
2 Are newcomers invited and welcomed to social events?					
3 Do you see social events as a place to get to know new people in church?					
4 Do you regularly hold special newcomers' events where they can find out about the church and meet the leaders?					
5 Does the notice sheet always have clear and up-to-date information about events?					
6 Are events always advertised clearly for everyone, with a poster?					
7 Does your Welcome Booklet let everyone know what's happening?					
8 Are you a friendly church where newcomers get invited to things that are happening?					
9 Does your church ever go away for the day or for a weekend away?					
10 Does your church ever do communal meals, perhaps after a Sunday service?					
Your Score out of 30 =					

An average score of 20 or more suggests your church is doing pretty well in this area. Under 20, and you might want to revisit your answers to see where improvements might be made in this general area. Any individual item scoring 1 or 0 may also need highlighting for improvement.

What can you do to improve the church's community life for new people?

Session 4: Belonging

Session 4: Belonging
to the church community

3 Christian nurture

Questions	Yes/Good 3 points	OK/ Satisfactory 2 points	Could be better 1 point	No/Poor 0 points	Total points
1 Does your church regularly run a nurture course?					
2 Are new people personally invited to the nurture course?					
3 Does the course you run suit the type of people new to your church?					
4 Do you advertise the course to outsiders?					
5 Is the course you run attractive to the people in your neighbourhood?					
6 Is the venue of your course suitable?					
7 Do you have a team involved in running the course?					
8 Do you use a meal or some other way to encourage friendships?					
9 Is the time(s) of year you hold it strategically chosen or ad hoc?					
10 Do you have anything for people to attend following the nurture course?					
Your Score out of 30 =					

An average score of 20 or more suggests your church is doing pretty well in this area. Under 20, and you might want to revisit your answers to see where improvements might be made in this general area. Any individual item scoring 1 or 0 may also need highlighting for improvement.

a Do you think the church needs to start a nurture course or change the way in which nurture of new people happens?

b What happens after your nurture course?

Session 4: Belonging
to the church community

4 Pastoral care

Questions	Yes/Good 3 points	OK/ Satisfactory 2 points	Could be better 1 point	No/Poor 0 points	Total points
1 Do you have an effective pastoral care team and not leave it all to the minister?					
2 Are new people quickly integrated into fellowship groups or the normal supportive structures?					
3 Do your small groups care for most people in the church?					
4 Have you carefully thought through your pastoral care networks?					
5 Are people missed when they stop coming and is something done about it?					
6 Are newcomers routinely invited to join home groups or cells?					
7 Do you have other small groups where newcomers may be loved and cared for? (e.g. choir, bellringers)					
8 As a church do you think you take pastoral care very seriously and make sure you do it well?					
Your Score out of 24 =					

An average score of 16 or more suggests your church is doing pretty well in this area. Under 16, and you might want to revisit your answers to see where improvements might be made in this general area. Any individual item scoring 1 or 0 may also need highlighting for improvement.

Are newcomers well cared for? How easy is it for them to slip away from regular attendance unnoticed? Does anyone notice if they stop coming and does anyone do anything? If so, who?

Session 4: Belonging

Session 4: Belonging
to the church community

5 Christian service

Questions	Yes/Good 3 points	OK/ Satisfactory 2 points	Could be better 1 point	No/Poor 0 points	Total points
1 Does your church encourage everyone to use their gifts?					
2 Do you have a way of helping people to explore their gifts to find their right area of service?					
3 Are there clear job descriptions for roles in your church?					
4 Is there a probationary period and time limit for jobs in the church?					
5 Do the people who do jobs feel affirmed and valued?					
6 Does your church have teaching about gifts and service?					
7 Do you get to know newcomers as people before asking them to take on jobs?					
8 Are people asked to do anything in church without having to wait years to be approached?					
Your Score out of 24 =					

An average score of 16 or more suggests your church is doing pretty well in this area. Under 16, and you might want to revisit your answers to see where improvements might be made in this general area. Any individual item scoring 1 or 0 may also need highlighting for improvement.

How easy do you think it would be for a newcomer to get involved in an area of service in your church?

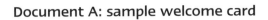

Document A: sample welcome card

St Agatha's

Welcome! Please only fill in the bits you don't mind giving information about.

Name _____

Address _____

_____ Postcode _____

Tel: _____

Email _____

Do you already go to a church?

☐ Yes ☐ No ☐ Sometimes

If 'yes', which church? _____

☐ If you would you like to know more about St Agatha's, please tick this box

☐ If you would you like to know more about Christianity, please tick this box

Please return this to a member of Staff or send it to

Revd J. Vicar, St Agatha's Vicarage, Church Lane, Churchtown CH1 0EW.

Document B: sample welcome letter

Dear

It was good to see you on Sunday at St Agatha's. I hope you enjoyed the service. I have enclosed for you a copy of the 'Welcome Booklet' which explains most of what takes place at St Agatha's.

We have a variety of types of services and various midweek activities and groups for people to become involved in. Our policy is that you are welcome to everything but we don't twist your arm to come to anything! If you would like to know more about any of the items in the booklet please ask us when you come again or phone me.

For those enquiring about the Christian faith, we have '_____'. This is a _____ week course designed to help people understand more about the Christian faith. It is also good as a 'refresher' for those who have been involved in Christianity before. We also run 'Start!' and 'Essence' and one of the three mentioned courses will be starting after Easter if you are interested.

We'd love to see you again and I look forward to hopefully you coming again in the near future. If you need to chat about anything, please give me a ring on _____.

God bless you,

_____ Vicar

Document C: sample pastoral care register

	October					November				December				Notes:
	02	09	16	23	30	06	13	20	27	04	11	18	25	
9.30 Regular														
Cobley, Tom														
Cole, King														
Horner, Jack														
Hubbard, Mother														
Sprat, Jack														
9.30 Occasional														
Foster, Doctor														
Lamb, Mary														
Thumb, Tom														
11.15 New/Visitors														
Whittington, Dick														

Session 4: Belonging

Training

a Welcome Team

■ Contents ■

■ Session 5 aim ■

The aim of this session is to create a Welcome Team appropriate to the needs of your church situation and to look at the ongoing development of that team.

■ Session 5 outline ■

Welcome Housekeeping notices and prayer .... 4 minutes

Just for fun The worst things people could say to a newcomer .... 5 minutes

Word on welcome Reading: Matthew 25.34-45 (abridged) with brief
comment .... 6 minutes

Mystery worshipper experience .... 5 minutes

Sample exercise 1 What does a Welcome Team do before a service? .... 10 minutes

Sample exercise 2 What does a Welcome Team do after a service? .... 10 minutes

Discussion The role of the Welcome Team in our church .... 20 minutes

Ongoing meetings and training Discuss what is needed in your context .. 15 minutes

So what do we do next? Sharing ideas .... 10 minutes

Course Prayer .... 5 minutes

■ Session 5 leaders' notes ■

There is no material in the Members' Manual for this session and so the notes needed by the group will have to be photocopied. You will need to print off sufficient copies of the sample guidelines in Additional Notes E (page 134).

Welcome Even though this is a smaller group specifically invited, still ensure there is a good welcome for them. Open the meeting in prayer, probably using the Course Prayer said together.

Just for fun Use the Additional Notes Exercise 6b on page 136 to introduce this session. In groups of three or four collect the worst things that could be said to a new person. Share them in a big group. Sometimes they are painfully not so far from what people do say.

Word on welcome Matthew 25.34-45 (for abridged version see page 116). Brief comment: these are stern words from Jesus. Too many people come to our churches and find, 'When I was as stranger ... you ignored me'. We are developing a Welcome Team in order to try to ensure that everyone who comes into our church is welcomed in Jesus' name on the day and also invited into the community of the church subsequently.

Mystery worshipper experience Either read the account about Easter Sunday morning (page 113) or tell a story of your own to remind everyone of the need for welcome.

Sample exercise 1 Use the notes from Area 3 (page 121) about what a Welcome Team does before a service. Do this as a general exercise with the whole group and use it to clarify how your team will operate in your situation, whether they will be part of an existing sidespersons' team, which has its role extended, or exist as a separate team.

Sample exercise 2 Use the notes from Area 5 (page 122 about 'Experience after a service'). Introduce it by briefly referring back to the Everybody Welcome Course (Session 3, Aspect 4), then stimulate discussion by asking the question: 'What does the Welcome Team need to do for the newcomer after the service has ended?' If you have a large group, divide it into teams of three or four for discussion and then relate answers back to the whole group. Collate the answers on paper or on a flip chart and at the end have a series of action points for you as a Welcome Team and, if relevant, to put to your church's leadership team.

Discussion The role of the Welcome Team in your church. Hand out the sample guidelines in Additional Notes E (page 134), but make it clear from the outset that the aim of this section is to look at what would be appropriate for your Welcome Team, not to impose these guidelines on them. Discuss the guidelines and make appropriate changes for your situation.

Session 5: Training

Ongoing meetings and training Discuss the need to meet regularly to sustain the team. We recommend at least three times a year to discuss individuals, have ongoing training and provide mutual support. Discuss what is appropriate in your context and set the dates of the meetings for the coming year.

So what do we do next? Ask people to share how they are feeling about this. There may be some who are ready to sign up immediately; others who have decided this is not for them and cannot wait to escape; yet others who want time to think and pray about this ministry. Do not force people to say what they feel but make it possible for those who wish to do so.

You will also need to fix a deadline by which individuals commit to joining the Welcome Team or decide to opt out. Once the membership of the team has been fixed you will probably need to have a second meeting at which a number of practicalities can be arranged, including:

- when the team should start its ministry
- how it should be launched
- badges and rotas
- exact job description for team members
- relationship with sidespeople
- reporting and meeting arrangements.

You might also go through another unit or two of the training suggested below.

End Thank everyone for coming and close in prayer.

Leaders' introduction

There are three crucial parts to the creation and development of a Welcome Team which these notes will help you with:

- selecting the right people
- establishing clear guidelines for your church situation so the team know what they are doing
- creating structures for ongoing development and support.

This session presumes that many of your congregation members have completed the Everybody Welcome Training Course and the overall ethos of the church is increasingly one of Welcome. The aim of the Welcome Team is not to do all the welcoming and push everybody else out but to assist and enable the whole congregation in the process of welcome. Those you have invited to be part of the Welcome Team also need to have completed Sessions 1–4.

This session is a very practical one where the minister will work with the Welcome Team to begin to establish the best way to work in your situation. It is only an initial meeting and the key to the success of a Welcome Team is the ongoing meetings. There are plenty of materials in this session that can be used for the ongoing training rather than this initial meeting. There are no materials for this session in the Members' Manual and so you may wish to buy a copy of the Leaders' Manual for every member of the Welcome Team, or else ask them to buy their own. This will not only enable them to work through Session 5 with you but also provide them with a reference book they can continue to look at as they gain experience in being welcomers.

Before we move to specific training ideas, here is a reminder of why we need Welcome Teams.

Every church will say, 'We're a friendly church.' Unfortunately, the people who visit our churches do not find that to be the case. This is the story of what happened to someone who visited two churches as a 'mystery worshipper'.

One Easter Sunday morning I visited two churches as a 'mystery worshipper'. At the first one the vicar was at the bottom of the drive welcoming people at the gate – impressive! I walked up the drive and there was a note on the door saying to use the door further round. I walked on – to find that I was walking on gravestones – not a pleasant thought. In addition to this, the stones became very uneven and so there was now a health and safety problem.

When I got to the door and opened it there was a curtain across the inside of the door which I had to pull to one side – it was like going through the wardrobe into Narnia. Unfortunately, inside it wasn't quite as beautiful as Narnia but quite dark and foreboding. I took

my books, as you do, and someone the other side of the aisle held out their hand to shake mine. I shook hands with them – but as I did I realized they had not been looking towards me but someone else, who they continued to look towards even while shaking my hand. I sat down and nobody apart from the vicar spoke to me, until the Peace. The service was OK. The hymns were fairly dull but the vicar's sermon was excellent. I left as soon as I had received communion as I wanted to go to another church.

I arrived at the second church late. I entered feeling very self-conscious and hastened towards the nearest available pew and sat down. I looked round and suddenly realized that those seated round me were in robes – yes, I'd sat in the choir! In that church the choir sit at the back of the church. Thankfully they did not sing an anthem so I was OK. During the Peace the choir were friendly towards me but the old lady in the row behind me did nothing but grumble and complain about everything in that service so far. I thought the service was quite good but the sermon was rather lightweight – about Easter Bunnies. At the end nobody spoke to me. I even tried the 'little boy lost' look and stood around for a while but still nobody spoke. It was a long journey home and so I looked around for some toilets but could see no signs about them. I gave up and left, and there was not even anyone on the door shaking hands with people.

When I wrote to the vicar I suggested they had drinks at the end of the service as this would be good for outsiders. He replied that they did have drinks – but he hadn't mentioned it in the notices and nobody invited me! If I was a newcomer, would I go to that church again?

Sadly, far too often, visitors to our churches are not welcomed. In a small family church it may be easy to spot the newcomer but the strength of relationship between those who are regulars may be so strong that it is virtually impossible for the stranger to break in. In a larger congregation, or a church with multiple congregations, people do not know each other well and so they are afraid of welcoming someone who has been coming longer than they have! The result is that the stranger does not find it easy to integrate into our churches. Many churches have found that they have to be 'intentional' about their welcome and not leave it to chance or the general friendliness of the congregation. They develop a team of welcomers.

In an ideal world, or rather an ideal church, a Welcome Team is not necessary because everyone who comes is welcomed so warmly by everybody. In the real world, and real churches, it is not quite as easy. The Welcome Team is a safety net to notice and catch the ones that aren't naturally welcomed; they've developed a bit of know-how in making people feel at ease and getting their contact details; and they provide the continuity of keeping an eye on the new people as they integrate into the church. If others do it, that's great; if not, the Welcome Team are there to make sure someone does it.

Even churches that succeed in giving a warm welcome to someone during and after a Sunday service often fall down when it comes to the much harder business of helping newcomers or enquirers integrate into the community of the church and begin to belong. The key concept of the Welcome Team is that it aims to welcome people not just at the point of attendance at church services but into membership of the church family. Here is another true story:

> After years of being a vicar I moved to a non-parish job so my wife and I looked for a new church to attend. For four months we attended a nearby church and relaxed in the congregation. Some people were friendly to us during and after the service, though most never spoke to us. Then I said to the vicar, 'I've had a rest now, I'll take a service for you if you like.' A couple of weeks later I led a communion service. Shaking hands on the way out several people thanked me for visiting them today. For four months I had been totally invisible to these good Christian people! No wonder that we had not been invited to anyone's home or to any church events or groups. We eventually realized that we were not going to find a route from attending the service to joining the church community, and in fact we began to wonder whether there was any church community anyway! So we left and joined another church where we could join a cell group, make friends, and find people who would pray with us. It was not the lack of welcome on Sundays that drove us away, it was the lack of ability of the church to absorb us into its life and community.

So the responsibility of the Welcome Team is to be the route into the heart and hospitality of the church such that newcomers would not dream of drifting away from their new friends and soul-mates.

As you gain experience you will need to work out how long a newcomer's welfare in the church remains the responsibility of the Welcome Team and when they can be considered to have arrived as a regular congregation member. Different people will proceed at different rates so there may be no one time period that fits all. However, the Welcome Team should always watch out for people during the whole of their first six months. It is good practice after someone has been coming for a few months for the minister or other leader to talk to the new member about how they are fitting in, what their aspirations are, and what sort of role they would like in the church. This would also be a good opportunity to discern what, if any, future help the Welcome Team can be to that person.

In creating and sustaining a Welcome Team there are certain key principles that apply in all situations. However, the way in which these principles are put into action will vary according to the individual church situation. In view of this, it is important for each church to think carefully through its own needs and situation.

Session 5: Training

Throughout this Session, we use the term 'Welcome Team', but we realize that 'welcome' will operate differently in different church settings; some smaller churches will have one key person plus a deputy; other churches will expand their sidespersons teams; yet others will create a separate designated group. The term 'Welcome Team' covers all these different ways of doing the job of welcome.

It is important to keep in mind that in this process we are looking at ways in which we, as the church, can reflect God's welcoming heart to the people whom he loves. High importance is placed on welcome in the teaching of Jesus.

> **Then the King will say to those on his right, 'Come, you who are blessed by my Father; take your inheritance, the kingdom prepared for you since the creation of the world. For ... I was a stranger and you invited me in ...' Then the righteous will answer him, 'Lord, when did we see you ... a stranger and invite you in ... ?' The King will reply, 'I tell you the truth, whatever you did for one of the least of these brothers of mine, you did it for me.' Then he will say to those on his left, 'Depart from me, you who are cursed, into the eternal fire prepared for the devil and his angels. For ... I was a stranger and you did not invite me in ...'. They also will answer, 'Lord, when did we see you ... a stranger ... and did not help you?' He will reply, 'I tell you the truth, whatever you did not do for one of the least of these, you did not do for me.'**
>
> **(Matthew 25.34–45, abridged)**

First of all, it is important to talk about recruiting the right people for a Welcome Team as this is fundamental to the whole process. This needs to have been done well in advance of this session so that the right people are invited.

Setting up and recruiting a Welcome Team

a Setting up a Welcome Team

This needs to be done after discussion and agreement with the Leadership/PCC of the church.

Decide whether you are going to use one or two individuals, extend the sidespersons team or set up a separate team. There are benefits and difficulties whichever way you do it, but it is important to be clear from the beginning. If you use and extend your present sidesperson team, then there may be those on the present team who have taken that role for all sorts of reasons and they may not be the best 'welcomers'. If you create a separate team then this may cause resentment and competition, especially if it is not clear what each of their responsibilities is. If you take the time and trouble to work out what you feel the job description of the Welcome Team is, this will help you to clarify the above question. There are some helpful guidelines for the sidesperson in Additional Notes B. It is important for you to clarify what type of team is best for your church.

b Recruiting a Welcome Team

A general request in the notices asking for volunteers is not the best way to develop a good team. You might end up with a team consisting of these:

- the shy person who wants to do this so they can make new friends – but the problem is that they don't know how to make conversation
- the gushing person who hugs everything that moves
- the rabid evangelist whose personality type tends to be insensitive.

The best way is for the minister and leadership team to get together and prayerfully think through which people to invite. You may need to choose some of your best members for this ministry and take them out of other roles! Here are some qualities to look for:

- Pastoral awareness and sensitivity. They need to be able to spot the outsider (so know who the regulars are) and know when to back off and not push the outsider beyond where they want to go.
- People-person skills. Someone who can instigate and sustain conversations and can think on their feet when engaging with people. Lack of conversation is very embarrassing for everyone. You don't need to do a Myers-Briggs personality profile on possible candidates, but you do need someone who is naturally outgoing, relaxed and sociable.
- Commitment. Being on the Welcome Team may involve being there early enough to notice and say hello to new people, being willing to miss the first part of the service as they will need to be on hand at the back to welcome late-comers, staying around at the end to take people for refreshments and make sure they are OK as they leave. If you develop a rota for being on duty, it is important to be willing to help and befriend on other weeks also rather than having the attitude, 'I'm not on duty this week!'
- If you have a large team, try to get a cross-section of ages and gender. If your priority is to attract particular people-groups to a particular service (for example, young families at the 10.30 a.m. service) then at least some of the Welcome Team should be those sorts of people. Like attracts like.

The reason why it is important to be so careful about this area of ministry is that newcomers arrive with different expectations and desires. They may include:

- the person visiting relatives who live nearby but who is used to church
- the person trying church for the first time, having tried various New Age remedies
- the person in a crisis and desperately needing help and a shoulder to cry on
- the person who had a funeral last week and so now wants to try church
- the marriage couple
- the baptism couple

to name but a few ...

And within each of these categories, you have different character traits, which means no one can be treated the same. Here are two typical reactions:

> I sat at the back of the church and a member of the congregation who was sitting near me found the pages for me. I mentioned that I was not confirmed and could not receive communion. He insisted that I went to be blessed by the priest ... the emotion I felt on being blessed was overwhelming.
>
> (56-year-old teacher)

> The last thing I want when I go to church is a gushing person at the door who insists on shaking my hand and asking me a whole string of questions about myself.
>
> (recently bereaved widower)

You will never get it right all the time, but you do want to avoid at all costs the story which is all so familiar: 'I went to that church but no one spoke to me ...' or 'The vicar came and spoke but no one else seemed interested ...' or, recently overheard, 'For the first two years only the clergy spoke to us.'

Having a Welcome Team is one of the ways to make sure that this wall of silence does not freeze people out from joining your church.

Organizing and sustaining a Welcome Team

We suggest the following guidelines for the role of the Welcome Team. Members should:

- befriend new people and gather information about them (this information needs to be written down).
- help newcomers develop friendships in the church by introducing them to others, inviting them to events where they can meet others etc.
- encourage newcomers to join a nurture group and, later, to follow this on into a small group.
- have the primary responsibility for contacting people if they stop attending – or making sure someone does.

It is important to have one key person who coordinates this area of work. The role of the Welcome Team Coordinator is to ensure that they or someone else:

- collate the information gathered about visitors: e.g. contact details, updating them as necessary. Document A (page 105) is an example of useful information to keep either on a card or database.
- keep a pastoral care list of the attendance of new people so that follow-up can be done in case someone is ill. See Document B (page 106) for a sample of a pastoral care list for new people.
- coordinate with those responsible for pastoral care to hand over the care of an individual at the relevant time.
- allocate to individual members of the Welcome Team primary responsibility for one or more new people to ensure individuals are not missed out.

The Coordinator will need to call the team together to meet regularly. These meeting should be at least three times a year. There are three key elements to a typical meeting:

■ discussion of individuals (within confidentiality boundaries): exchanging information, considering the best way to help them to integrate, and making recommendations for those who will be moved over to the pastoral care team.

■ ongoing training. Take a specific area and do some ongoing training using materials from this session or the web site. Use these to review and update your procedures.

■ mutual support and care: sharing good and bad experiences, praying for each other and the work of the team.

You need to decide how to organize the team. There are various possibilities:

■ a smaller team who have this as their primary responsibility in the church and are on duty every week.

■ a larger team that operates a rota with people on duty one week per month.

■ a larger team that operates a rota where team members are on duty for a month at a time as this helps consistency.

If you rota your team members there needs to be an agreement that welcoming is about people, not rotas, so that newcomers are not ignored just because a potential welcomer is not 'on duty'.

A 'Welcome Desk' can be a useful focus for the work of the Welcome Team and provide a point of approach for the newcomer. In some churches it is simply a place where all the leaflets, information and pens are kept, while in others there is always someone present to talk to people who approach it. Much of this depends on the size of the church, both in terms of the number of people and the physical space available.

Identity badges can be very useful for a Welcome Team. A badge can seem rather impersonal but in an age where people are increasingly suspicious, it can give reassurance to the newcomer and confidence to the team member. This explanation was found on one church's web site:

> We hope that visitors to Gushing Waters Baptist Church will find everyone friendly and welcoming but each Sunday we have a small team of people who make a special effort to help out. You can spot who they are because they will be wearing their Welcome Team badges.

Materials to use for training the Welcome Team

These materials cannot all be used in this opening training session but they provide subjects for ongoing training, vital for the development of the ministry of the Welcome Team.

When you have a training session introduce the subject by referring back to the initial course, and perhaps ask team members to read some relevant pages from the Leaders' Manual. Then initiate discussion using the 'Over to you' question(s) suggested, or those of your own. If you have a large group you may find it best to divide up into smaller groups of three or four people for discussion then relate back to the whole group. Collate the ideas on paper or on a flip chart and at the end have a series of action points for you as a Welcome Team and, if relevant, to put to your church's leadership team.

What does a Welcome Team do? The areas are:

1   Discover

2   Experience of the premises

3   Experience before a service

4   Experience during a service

5   Experience after a service

6   Belong: personal friendship

7   Belong: community life

8   Belong: Christian nurture

9   Belong: pastoral care

10   Belong: Christian service

11   Should someone visit?

12   The door welcomer

13   Obtaining people's contact details

14   Sample guidelines for a Welcome Team member

15   Exercises.

Area 1: Discover

Ask your group to think back to the first part of the Everybody Welcome Course. It looked at all the contacts you have with people who do not come to church. In some churches there is a Mission Team or an Outreach Team with responsibility for engaging with these contacts and providing a link with the church. In fact people who join a Welcome Team are likely to be part of any such group. If your church has such a group, then this area will be dealt with by them; if your church does not have such a group, then this is an area to consider.

> ### Over to you ...
>
> **What are some of the ways in which the Welcome Team could help the church to engage with those who use our buildings so they take the next step into church?**

Some of the areas a Welcome Team could engage in are:

- Organizing a 'Back to Church Sunday'
- Providing invitations to special services and events for the congregation members to use with their contacts

- Ensuring there is good publicity for special services and events
- Encouraging ways in which hall users can be made aware of church events and be invited
- Developing the church's web site as a tool not only for marketing the church but also for keeping everyone in touch.

Area 2: Experience of the premises

Refer back to the second session of the Everybody Welcome Course.

Over to you ...

Walk into the church, putting yourself in the shoes of an outsider. Are there ways in which you can improve the welcome for newcomers? Are there recommendations to be made to the leadership of the church?

Some of the areas a Welcome Team could engage in or instigate are:

- Work parties to improve the grounds
- Investigating provision for special needs and disability groups
- Suggesting a re-design of the welcome desk or the circulating space to make them more user-friendly.

Area 3: Experience before a service

Our reaction to something is often coloured by the first 60 seconds of the experience. Think through some of the areas you need to look out for *before* the service, remembering that one of your main tasks is to do all you can to reduce 'anxiety' in the newcomer.

Over to you ...

How can the Welcome Team help to reduce the anxiety levels of the newcomer when they first come into church?

Some of the areas that will have arisen are listed below, but there will be some things peculiar to your church:

- The door may be a barrier and needs a person on it to open it and welcome people.
- If the Welcome Team is part of the Sidesperson Team you may wish to discuss aspects of this here: e.g. the number of books given out, the place the sidespersons stand etc.
- Newcomers may be unsure where to sit. Look out for this and show them to a suitable seat. Watch out especially for any disabled people here.
- Do all you can to make newcomers feel at ease. If no one else has done so, introduce yourself and give your name, ask for theirs and check that they have all they need for the service. You will normally be able to tell whether they want to talk further or want to be left alone.

Session 5: Training

- It is often helpful to point out to them where the toilets are and that there are refreshments afterwards – chat further there if they wish to.

- If you discover they are unused to church, you may decide to sit near them to help them with the service. If it is a communion service, you perhaps need to explain a bit about this, and the option of receiving a blessing if appropriate. (You may also need to explain 'the Peace'.)

Area 4: Experience during a service

You are so used to church yourself that you easily forget the anxieties that a newcomer can have during a service.

> ### Over to you ...
> **What can the Welcome Team do to help a newcomer during a service?**

Here are some of the areas to consider:

- Be ready to help if newcomers cannot find where they are in the service (gently and unobtrusively, so as not to show them up).

- If it is a communion service and the Peace is shared in the service, this can be the most excruciating and isolating time for any stranger, even those who are full members of another church. Be alongside and introduce them to others who come to you. Or if they are shy and retiring, try to protect them.

- Watch out in case they leave early. There may be all sorts of reasons for this and for someone to follow and check they are OK can be crucial. It may be that they didn't realize the service lasted as long as it does and need to get home. If they leave and no one goes to them, they will probably never ever come back because they are too embarrassed. It may be that they are in crisis and something upset them – if they leave and no one talks, they will be too embarrassed to come back; if someone does check they are OK, they can often be helped.

Area 5: Experience after a service

This can be the most difficult time for any newcomer, who can be either left alone to fend for themselves or be engulfed by well-meaning enthusiasts.

> ### Over to you ...
> **What does the Welcome Team need to do for the newcomer after the service has ended?**

Some of the suggestions which should arise from the group are:

- Invite the newcomer for refreshments after the service and accompany them, especially if this is in another building.

- Don't charge for refreshments – this gives a terrible impression. The word 'donations' is even worse as the stranger will not know what to give. Have a budget for tea, coffee and biscuits and, where possible, use Fair Trade (people notice these things these days).

- Inform them about other church activities so they know what else is happening. It is helpful to have a leaflet outlining these for them to take away with them. If appropriate, invite them to:
  - a nurture course
  - a newcomers' event
  - other services (e.g. midweek, alternative style)

- Introduce them to others who you feel they might get on with. Don't create a dependence on yourself. As gratifying as that is, you will then cease to be free to welcome others.

- Try to get contact details from them (see Additional Notes C).

- Continue to keep an eye out for them even if you have introduced them to others as they may leave and the newcomer be left alone again.

Area 6: Belong: personal friendship

If a newcomer does not make several significant new personal friendships in the church, they are not likely to stay.

Over to you ...

How can the Welcome Team help newcomers to forge significant new friendships within the church?

- Introduce newcomers to regular members not only the first week but also on subsequent weeks.

- Make it easier for the regular member by reminding them of the name of the person they spoke to last week and pointing out that they are here again.

- Sometimes the welcomer herself or himself might personally befriend the newcomers.

Area 7: Belong: community life

Over to you ...

What can the Welcome Team do to ensure social events are a place where new people can integrate into the life of the church?

- Make sure newcomers have been invited to the next social event either by inviting them yourself or checking that the person you introduced them to has invited them. It is often best to arrange to meet someone or pick them up and go with them to the event.

Session 5: Training

- Ensure that the publicity for social events is clear and accessible to all. If your church has a social committee which arranges and publicizes these events, then all well and good. If your church does not have an organizer or good publicity, it might be that the Welcome Team see this as part of their role to help the newcomers to integrate into the life of the church and make friendships.

Area 8: Belong: Christian nurture

Over to you ...

How can nurture courses be used most effectively for newcomers in your church?

- Ensure that each new person has been invited to the nurture course well in advance of it.
- If your church does not have a nurture group, it may be the Welcome Team who need to instigate this.
- Offer to go with the newcomer to the first couple of meetings.
- The Achilles heel of most nurture courses is what happens afterwards. In some churches this is handled well but in others it is left to the individual. Having been introduced to a small group through the nurture course, many will want to continue this but do not presume they will just find a small group for themselves. Here the Welcome Team need to keep an active interest in the new person to ensure that they do not slip through the net at this point.

Area 9: Belong: pastoral care

Over to you ...

What is needed in your church to ensure new people do not slip through the pastoral net?

- If a person has suddenly stopped attending, the Welcome Team need to make contact.
- Look at what systems you need to spot who is missing. Do you need a pastoral care attendance sheet? (see Document B).
- Sometimes the person may have decided that they do not wish to attend any more. In this case we need to respect their decision and not put undue pressure on them.

Area 10: Belong: Christian service

Over to you ...

Do you think people should be asked as soon as possible to do a job or should we wait until they are integrated into the church? Who should ask them?

- Is your church open to new people getting involved? If not, you might need to consider ways in which you can help it to change.

- Keep a note of interests, skills and experience that come up in conversation with the new person. At the appropriate time, refer these on to the relevant people, e.g. you may find out someone loves singing, so when it is appropriate you may pass their name to the choir or worship leader.

- Explore possible courses that look at people's gifts and how to use them in the church.

Area 11: Should someone visit?

In some churches there is a deliberate attempt to visit each newcomer. Additional Notes D shows some interesting research on this. Photocopy this and use it as a basis for discussion.

> **Over to you ...**
>
> **Do you think the American research (see Additional Notes p. 133) is applicable to our country and your community? Do you think you should make home visits to newcomers and, if so, when?**

- In some communities, a visit might be appropriate; in others a phone call is more acceptable.

- In youth culture, a text message or email is culturally relevant.

- The important thing is to get across the message, 'We care about you.'

Area 12: The door welcomer

Provide photocopies of Additional Notes A for everyone to read.

> **Over to you ...**
>
> **How important is it to have a member of the Welcome Team welcoming people at the door?**

Area 13: Obtaining people's contact details

Additional Notes C shows why it is vital to obtain people's contact details.

> **Over to you ...**
>
> **What are the difficulties in obtaining people's contact details? What have you found to be the best way to do it? Can you improve?**

Area 14: Sample guidelines for a Welcome Team member

Use the draft in Additional Notes E or one of your own as a basis for discussion. We strongly recommend that you develop guidelines for your Welcome Team and keep

Session 5: Training

them under review.

Over to you ...

Have a look at the draft guidelines for a Welcome Team member. How do these need to be adapted for your situation?

OR

Read and review your Welcome Team guidelines. Do any changes need to be made?

Area 15: Exercises

It is good to incorporate practical exercises and role plays into your ongoing training (see Additional Notes F).

Over to you ...

Use one of the training ideas from Additional Notes F to improve your skills and sensitivity.

And finally

We want the whole congregation to be welcoming! Of course we do. We are simply recognizing in setting up a Welcome Team that a good welcome does not always come naturally, that it is good to have some people with a special responsibility and training for this vital ministry. The Welcome Team are there to assist the whole congregation to be welcoming and to be the safety net when needed. The Welcome Team should be delighted if the general members of the congregation welcome newcomers before they do (but if you spot someone doing this regularly, invite them onto the Welcome Team).

It is important to have this ministry of welcome recognized and for people to understand what the role is. A good way of doing this is to have a commissioning service for the Welcome Team. The congregation need to understand that the Welcome Team will be introducing newcomers to them and that their role is to offer acceptance and friendship as they are able.

Additional notes A: the door welcomer

The need for a door welcomer

Spend some time watching your main door(s). Look at any problems people may have when they arrive at church. Try especially to look at it from the standpoint of an outsider.

- Can you see the interior of the church from outside the door? If you have a big wooden door, like most churches do, then consider having a friendly person on the outside of the door to welcome people and open the door for them (they'll need a coat in winter).

- How do people who are disabled cope with your entrance? Look at it from the viewpoint of a wheelchair user. If they come alone in a motorized wheelchair, how long might they have to wait to be able to get in? Perhaps another reason to have someone on the door.

- When the door is opened, does it slam shut on the next person? This can be very embarrassing, especially if the person is late.

- Are there steps? How do elderly people or indeed anybody unsteady on their feet cope?

Of course, if your door has glass in it then the welcomer can stand inside and watch out for people and open the door at an appropriate time.

The role of the door welcomer

The door welcomer's role is to offer a friendly face, a warm greeting and a handshake, and to make sure people can get through the door(s) easily.

Recruitment and training

Do not simply ask for volunteers and hope for the best. It's just not true to say, 'Anyone is better than no one.' Some people find it very hard to smile! But also, you don't want someone who will hug every person who comes in, or engages people in long conversations or interrogations. The last thing you want is someone on the door who is actually putting people off as they arrive either by being unfriendly or being over-friendly.

Think carefully and prayerfully about who will do this job well. You may have one outstanding person who you ask to do it every week – but have a back-up in case they are ill or away. Or you may choose to have a team who each do it once a month.

Once you have selected your people, do an exercise with them, with you or others being the 'new person' and give plenty of feedback.

Do review this role and give plenty of encouragement.

Session 5: Training

Discussion points

1 Imagine the following people arriving outside your church, and put yourself in their shoes:

   a a person in a motorized wheelchair

   b an elderly couple, both infirm

   c a mother with a baby in a pram and a toddler in tow

   d a man who is desperate to find God but hesitant about church.

   What problems do you think they would encounter?

2 'Our doorway entrance is easy to get in; we don't need anyone on the door.' True or false? Give reasons for your answer.

3 Should you have one person welcoming on the door every week or a team so people do it once a month? What are the advantages and disadvantages?

4 What is the key role of the welcomer on the door?

Additional notes B: sidespersons

An important but underestimated role in churches is that of the sidesperson. Among their practical duties, they are one of the first people a newcomer will meet and so will make a lasting impression. Let's make sure it is a good impression. Good practice includes considering the following points:

a Look at where sidespersons are positioned. They need to be near enough to the entrance so newcomers are not left floundering but not so near that the entrance is too congested.

b If you have a large church with regular visitors, either have a large enough team so that individuals can take people to seats etc., or develop a separate 'Welcome Team'.

Tips for the welcomers

c Be there early enough to get the books and papers ready so that when people arrive you can give them confidently rather than fumbling trying to put everything together.

d Eye contact and a smile are important. The newcomer should not feel you have interrupted your conversation with your fellow sidesperson in order to speak to them.

e Treat everyone equally rather than engaging in a long conversation with someone and virtually ignoring everyone else.

f Be especially on the lookout for the newcomer, welcoming them and making sure they know where to go, and either take them yourself or hand them on to someone else.

In one church the new vicar noticed that, because of where the sidespersons sorted out their books and papers, they had their backs to the door where people came in. Over the years they had perfected the art of handing books to people over their backs while they continued to sort out the books and papers. The new vicar bought a small round table for £10, a plastic sign that said 'Welcome' and placed it just inside the door. The sidespersons now greet people as they come in and hand them their service books.

Discussion points

1 What is the main role of the sidesperson?

2 Give examples of the job done badly, and the job done well.

3 Are the sidespersons situated in the right place in your church?

4 What sorts of thing can help the sidespersons to do their job effectively and what things get in their way?

Session 5: Training

129

Additional notes C: obtaining people's contact details

Why is this important?

If a new person stops coming after two or three weeks (or six or seven) it may be for a very innocent reason like illness, but they invariably feel awkward about coming back. If you have no contact details you cannot get in touch with them. Also, if you want to invite them to something that is happening, you need to have their details.

How to do it

- Ask a question like: 'Do you live round here?' The reply often gives the road, in which case it is very easy to say, 'What number?' If they ask why, be honest: it's so you can invite them to anything that is happening and if they are ill and go missing you can check they are OK.

- Use a welcome card (see Additional Notes A for an example). Some churches find it easiest to have these in the pews/chairs and ask people to fill them in. People rarely fill them in without being asked – and someone needs to ensure they are always replenished. Every member of the Welcome Team should have some of these cards to hand.

- Send a welcome booklet. One church had a welcome booklet and instead of giving this to newcomers, they sent it to them with a simple letter of welcome from the vicar. Newcomers were asked: 'Please give us your contact details and we will send you the booklet.' It was simple and easy.

- Develop a list of those who have visited and have someone keep the list by collating the information from the welcome cards. This is especially important if you have more than one main service or a team of churches and the new person tries them all out!

People-types

You are probably dealing with two main types of visitor. The first type is a person new to the church, with little or no faith background. Very often they will prefer to remain anonymous so that they can retain control. The second type is the Christian who has moved into the area and is looking for a new church. You can often tell if someone is familiar with church by how they handle themselves in the service. In most cases these will want to be known and have a fuss made of them. Occasionally you might encounter someone who has been hurt in their last church and so wishes to remain anonymous. In all of these situations, pick up the clues and back off. Rarely will someone tell you directly that they do not want to give information about themselves. They are more likely to make excuses about needing to get home or escaping to the toilet. If, when you ask a question, they close it down immediately, then take the hint and do not push them. Also, look for body language. If the person avoids eye contact or shies away, respect their privacy.

P.S. Be realistic. Don't expect the Welcome Team to get all the names and addresses of all the visitors who come to a baptism! But they need to be on the lookout for the person who is new and not simply part of the baptism party.

Additional notes D: notes on visiting

Some interesting American research findings – how relevant do you think they are to the UK context?

The basic finding is summed up in the '36 hour principle': When lay persons visit the home of the first time worshipper within 36 hours, 85% of them will return to worship the next Sunday. When the visit is delayed for 72 hours, only 60% return; when delayed five to seven days, 15% return.

And the real shocker: If the vicar or minister makes the first visit, all of the percentages are cut in half – far fewer return. The reason is that the first time worshipper either feels that this is a paid duty the minister is performing, or the visitor is threatened by such a quick visit.

If the visit is made by a lay person or persons, however, the first-time worshipper feels 'The church must be important to them ... they care for me ... this must be a caring community.' The '36 hour principle' derives its power from two contextual factors.

First, there is the new 'church-shopper' mentality among American churchgoers. While half of the 16.6% of Americans who move each year stay in the same county or city and with the same church, of those who move farther away, half join a church of a different denomination.

Second, the feelings of loneliness and lack of connectedness among the American people accent the need for genuine interest and active caring. When a worshipper feels that concern, he or she will return.

What is the minister's role if they are not to make the visit? It is important for them to be involved.

He or she may:

- Mail a note to every guest who comes to worship.
- Meet for 15–20 minutes after worship every Sunday with the visitor coordinator to review the names of visitors.
- Telephone each local visitor within 36 hours to express appreciation and to get acquainted.
- Help develop in the entire congregation a consciousness of the presence of visitors and the importance of a friendly welcome.
- Help the evangelism committee recruit and train special visitors for worship guests.
- Be ready to visit when such a visit is desired.

Here are some suggestions for lay visitors:

- Stay no longer than 15–20 minutes.

- Do not telephone ahead – drop in and ask for just a few minutes. (If you question this procedure, try an experiment of ten visits with a telephone call and ten without.)

- Pray before each visit.

- Leave something from the church – a welcome booklet, a Prayer Book or New Testament. The Moravian tradition is to leave a 'sugar-cake'.

- If they are not at home, leave a brochure describing the church and a signed, hand-written note that says something like, 'Dear ..., Sorry we missed you. We were glad to have you in church. We hope you will come back Sunday'. Later in the week follow up with a phone call.

- Let future follow-up visits be made by trained evangelism callers.

Dr Erwin J. Kolb, *The Anglican Digest*, Late Pentecost 1988

Additional notes E: draft guidelines for a Welcome Team member

(This is a sample and will need to be modified for your situation)

1 Sunday duty responsibility:

a When on duty, arrive at least 20 minutes before a service to ensure that new people are welcomed. If they look as if they need help, take them to their seat and make them feel at home. Explain where the toilets are and anything about the service you think they might need to know (e.g. if it is communion, explain the Peace and the bread and wine).

b Wait until a few minutes after the service has begun to greet anyone who arrives late.

c During the service be sensitive to the needs of anyone who is new and watch in case they leave early. If so, check if they are all right but do not intrude on their privacy.

d At the end of the service befriend any new people and take them for refreshments. Sensitively try to obtain contact details. Make a note of their name somewhere so you do not forget it. Try to introduce them to others whom you think they might get on with. Keep an eye on them in case those you have introduced them to leave them on their own. Ensure they have any relevant information or invitations either to next week's service, social events or nurture course. If you have got their contact details pass them on to the Welcome Team Coordinator.

The following week, even if you are not 'on duty', keep an eye out for them and welcome them, trying to introduce them either to the same person as last week, or to someone new.

In the weeks that follow try to make sure:

a they are invited to any social events

b they are invited to any nurture course

c they are invited to any specific events to welcome newcomers

d they are followed up by you or someone else if they go missing.

2 Attend the meetings for support, follow-up and ongoing training three times a year.

Additional notes F: exercises

1 Feeling welcome

Using a flip chart, write up words and phrases under the following heading: 'I feel welcome when ...'. You might expect the following responses; draw out or suggest any key ones that are not mentioned.

I feel welcome when ...

- I have all the information I need
- I am not left to flounder about where to go or sit
- I can get into the building, find and use all its facilities
- I know where my children can be cared for
- People are friendly and helpful but not intrusive
- I can see and hear and move around as I need to
- I am not embarrassed by not knowing what to do
- I can join in with everything I would like to
- I don't feel awkward or conspicuous
- My cultural boundaries are not threatened
- I experience genuine hospitality
- I am not put under pressure
- I feel free to ask questions
- I am relaxed, not anxious or tense
- I can exercise choice and am not 'taken over'
- I am not too hot, cold, thirsty or physically uncomfortable
- Any physical contact is sensitive and appropriate
- I can communicate in my own language.

In a general discussion, the group explores the question: 'Why does welcoming people matter?' Look for both practical and theological thinking. We may hope that people will come back, but the underlying reason is that the gospel calls us to reflect the welcome God extends to all people.

2 Open questions

It is best to use open questions.

An open question is one that requires a full answer:

'What did you think of the service today?'

A closed question can be answered by a simple 'yes' or 'no':

'Did you enjoy the service?' 'Yes/No'

Open questions start with words like: How? What? Who? When? Where?

But remember, if people close down your questions, it might be that they do not wish to talk further.

Divide into twos and do role play in various situations and develop your skills at using open questions.

3 In other people's shoes

Either bring a variety of shoes to the meeting or drawings of different shoes. In groups of three or four, imagine the character of the person who has that shoe and then discuss how they may be welcomed into the life of the church at different stages, looking at the obstacles they will encounter and the way in which a Welcome Team can help them. Then each group in turn relate their ideas to the main group.

4 Gifting

In pairs – discuss what the members of the Welcome Team feel is their main gifting. Share your own gifting in the big group (this helps the course leader identify gifts and maybe pair people with opposite giftings on rotas etc.).

5 Walk through

Walk through (literally, from the outside door) a typical welcome with a volunteer 'new person' and get the group to add suggestions.

6 Listening skills

Choose from the following:

a Pairs work: five minutes each to speak on a topic. Each feeds back to the other the main points but also feelings they have picked up. Then they tell their partner how accurate it was (helps paraphrasing skills).

b Own self-awareness work: Draw a square on paper. In each corner answer one of the four questions: What strengths do I have as a listener? What things do I need to improve on? Is there a relationship where God is calling me to listen more? Who listens to me?

c Role play: one person is the newcomer. In groups of three, newcomer and welcomer have a conversation. Each 'new person' has been given a role on a piece of paper: e.g. very nervous, over-jolly etc. The third person observes. Then all three feedback what they thought was helpful/could be improved.

d Just for fun: course leaders demonstrate first how *not* to do it (make this funny), then how to do it. Those being trained list what is wrong/right in each case – and what can be improved in the good version too!

e In groups of three or four collect the *worst* things that could be said to a new person. Share them in the big group. Sometimes they are painfully close to the truth!

Document A: sample newcomer record card

Name _____

Address _____

_____ Postcode _____

Tel: _____ Email _____

Date of first contact _____

Details _____

_____

Nurture course _____

Small group _____

Service _____

Date handed on to Pastoral Care Team _____

Document B: sample pastoral care list

	October					November				December				Notes:
	02	09	16	23	30	06	13	20	27	04	11	18	25	
New Oct–Dec														
Cobley, Tom														
Cole, King														
Horner, Jack														
Hubbard, Mother														
Sprat, Jack														

Session 5: Training

137

Appendix

Welcome: the maths

Here is a spot of algebra that sheds light on the importance of welcome in the growth of churches.

The reasoning set out in this appendix demonstrates the key importance of the retention rate of newcomers for the growth of the churches. In summary, the algebra describes how church attendance this year equals last year's membership plus all of those who try us out who stick, less leavers, times their attendance frequency, plus visitors. When typical real-world numbers are inserted, we find that attendance moves very little in response to changes in the other factors but is much more responsive to changes in the retention rate. The main reason for this arithmetically is that real-world retention rates are so low.

> Average Weekly Attendance (A) is made up of those members (M) who turn up on an average week plus visitors (V).

By 'members' I don't mean some legal definition like 'people on the electoral roll'. I simply mean those who habitually attend at least sometimes, including those who are just starting to attend. In 'visitors' I include members of baptism parties, relatives of church members who happen to be visiting them, in fact anyone who is clear that they are a 'one-off' visitor rather than a candidate for belonging.

So we start with this little equation:

Equation 1 $A = fM + V$

Where f = the frequency with which members (M) attend. If everybody comes every week then the frequency proportion (f) is 1. If on average members come every other week then it is 0.5.

So all our first equation is saying is that average church attendance is determined by the number of members, by how often they come and by how many visitors turn up.

Church attendance has been going down in the UK since around 1960 because of falling M, f and V. But evidence from the periodic English Church Attendance Survey produced by Christian Research suggests that mostly it has been a mix of M and f in roughly equal measure. Put simply, half of the decline in attendance has been because there are fewer members and half because they come less often.

This algebra stuff doesn't really get any harder than that, so stay calm and carry on.

The next equation says that the change in membership (M) from last year (year 0) to this year (year 1) is equal to the number of joiners (J) less the number of leavers (L).

Equation 2 $M_1 - M_0 = J - L$

So the change in membership is the difference between the numbers who join and leave. But the number who join is not the same as the number of people who think about joining because not everyone who tries out a church actually joins it. In fact about 90% don't. So:

Equation 3 $J = rT$

Where T is the number of people who 'Try out' the church and r is the retention rate. It is the proportion of T who succeed in becoming part of M.

In most churches retention (r) is surprisingly small (about 0.1) and therein lies our main problem and our main opportunity.

So, now we can substitute rT in place of J in equation 2 because they are equal to each other:

Equation 4 $M_1 - M_0 = rT - L$

The change in members is that proportion of the people who try the church out who actually 'stick' minus the people who leave.

If we want to work out how many members there will be in year 1, we can use equation 5:

Equation 5 $M_1 = M_0 + rT - L$

The number of members in year 1 is membership last year plus that proportion of the people who try out the church who stick less the leavers.

We started out with equation 1 which said that:

$A = fM + V$

So, inserting 1s to indicate this year's figures, we get equation 6:

Equation 6 $A_1 = f_1 M_1 + V_1$

Now we know how to calculate M_1 from equation 5 so we can substitute the right-hand side of equation 5 for M_1 in equation 6 to give us:

Equation 7 $A_1 = f_1(M_0 + rT - L) + V_1$

So attendance this year is last year's membership plus all of those who try us out who stick, less leavers, times their attendance frequency, plus visitors.

So why did we need algebra to tell us that? Well, we didn't really, but it's a bit more than just a shorthand version for geeks. What we can do now is to put in some typical or average values for each factor and then see how changing one of them affects average attendance at a typical or average church.

So here are some values for a fairly typical church in the UK. Its total attendance starts at 70, with 60 members plus 10 visitors on an average week. This is slightly higher than the average Anglican church today, but once the rather larger Roman churches are included it may not be far off the current national average. With a frequency rate of 65% an average attendance of 60 members requires a membership of 93, so:

$M_0 = 93$

$f_0 = 0.65$

$V_0 = 10$

So, using equation 1 for Year 0 $A_0 = f_0 M_0 + V_0$

    $A_0 = 60 \ (0.65 \times 93) + 10 = 70$

So attendance in Year 0 = 70.

In an average year experience suggests that perhaps 8% of M move away, leave the church, die or become too incapacitated to attend. So L = 7.

This average church has been experiencing attendance decline of about two people a year, one due to lower attendance frequency (f) and one due to membership (M) going down. Attendance decline has slowed or stopped in many places recently, but let's assume the old long-term trend for the moment in order to understand what has been going on.

If L is 7 and the difference between L and J is 1 each year then we know that J must be 6.

But we also know from various pieces of research that r is somewhere around 0.1. The Church Life Survey in Australia suggests that there it is 0.08: that is, only 8% of people who try out a church become regular members. Experience of Back to Church Sunday in the UK suggests a similar figure, though one diocese making a big effort seems to have got the percentage up to about 13% (0.13 of those who try us out).

If r is 0.1 and J is 6 then we now know that there must have been 60 people trying the church out in some way during the year (T). One in ten of them stuck and the other nine did not.

This estimate of 60 people trying out the average church each year may seem very high to you. But just think how many people come to Christmas services – many of those 60 are probably coming in just two weeks at the end of the year. Others will come through bereavement, Back to Church Sunday, various other specific routes, plus the usual trickle of mystery people who just turn up once or twice then disappear. You may think that Christmas attenders should be classified as visitors (V) rather than people trying us out (T). But that is an attitude of mind. If Christmas attenders get a warm welcome and get invited back to other things there is a strong chance some of them will join. An attitude of mind that says that Christmas attenders are just one-off visitors is self-fulfilling.

The other half of average attendance decline is resulting from members coming less frequently. If f_0 is 0.65 then, roughly, f_1 will be 0.63, f_2 0.61 and so on. In year 0 the attendance of members is $0.65 \times 93 = 60$. In year 1 it is $0.63 \times 92 = 58$. Probably the number of visitors (V) is staying about the same (10) and so average attendance goes down from 70 to 68.

Equation 7 ($A_1 = f_1(M_0 + rT - L) + V_1$) showed us that if we want to grow average church attendance we need to do one or more of the following:

- increase attendance frequency, f
- increase the number of people who 'try us out', T
- increase their retention rate, r
- reduce the number of leavers, L
- increase the number of visitors, V.

We can now follow through the attendance changes that result from attempts at each of these five options in turn. We'll find out what happens when the number trying us out (T) doubles; when the trend in attendance frequency (f) is exactly reversed; when the number of people leaving (L) is reduced to the theoretical minimum; when the number of visitors (V) is doubled; and finally when the retention rate (r) is doubled.

So first of all let's have a major mission designed to get people interested in the faith and the church. Let's double the number of people who try us out: so T increases from 60 to 120. If $r = 0.1$ this increases J from 6 to 12. $J - L$ thus moves from -1 to $+5$. With 1 still being lost from average attendance through attendance frequency going down this results in a net increase in average attendance of 4: up from 70 to 74. The trouble is next year it will be down to 72 in the absence of another mission, and the year after back to 70 again. The underlying decline-trend has reasserted itself. The only impact on the figures is a small blip. No wonder missions have not been a good way of growing the church – they have been undone by the small retention rate and the reassertion of the long-term decline trend.

Second, let's try to improve attendance frequency. Let the vicar preach powerful sermons about 'Let us not give up meeting together, as some are in the habit of doing' (Hebrews 10.25). Knock out the unpopular services that people avoid, make the fortnightly service weekly, work at quality so that people will not want to be away in case they miss something.

Suppose you succeed in reversing the frequency trend such that f_1 (the proportion of weeks that people attend on average) becomes 0.67 instead of 0.63 and f_2 becomes 0.69 instead of 0.61, etc. This means that average attendance will rise by 1 per annum through frequency instead of falling by 1 per annum, and this will exactly match the decline in attendance brought about by declining membership. Attendance will remain at 70 each year. Decline has been stopped, but there is no overall growth. And eventually it becomes impossible to increase attendance frequency any more (there is a limit to how many weeks a year you can persuade people to attend – they are not going to cancel their holidays!) and the decline trend is bound to reassert itself.

So, thirdly, let's try to stop people leaving. This will involve so improving the health and pastoral care of the church community that no one would ever willingly leave. However, this will not stop people dying or becoming too ill to attend, or moving away because of job changes etc. So it will be possible to reduce L but not eliminate it. Suppose that you manage to get L down to its irreducible minimum – probably about 4 in the average church of 70. Now the membership will rise by a net 2 each year, and, with frequency still declining, attendance will rise by 1: 70 ... 71 ... 72 etc. Growth yes, but painfully slow. And the moment the guard is dropped and just one person leaves for no compelling reason growth disappears.

Okay, so fourthly, let's try to increase the number of visitors. Have lots of one-off events: invite various choirs to come and sing contributions, have the school in to lead a service and invite the parents, encourage baptism families to bring Uncle Tom Cobley and all. Suppose you manage, by dint of continuous hard work, to increase V from 10 to 20.

In Year 1 this will increase average attendance from 70 to 78 (without increasing V by 10 it would have gone down 2). But in Year 2 it will go down to 76, Year 3 to 74 and so on. And the instant that energy and ideas for attracting visitors falter numbers will go down further. You can't go on forever increasing the number of visitors.

I hope you are beginning to see why it is actually quite difficult to increase average church attendance in the UK these days – it's about as difficult as running up a down escalator. This does not mean it's impossible. When I was a child in the 1950s and the first department store with an escalator opened in the middle of Sheffield I delighted in achieving the feat, and evading the store staff in the process. The other day I tried it again and, indeed, found it a trifle harder than before, but still possible. I'm quite good for my age.

But there is a fifth option. Now work at increasing your retention rate (r). Prioritize the welcome of newcomers. Not just the handshake on the door but the integration into membership of the church community. Suppose you increase it from 0.1 to 0.2.

In that case then J becomes $60 \times 0.2 = 12$ so that M rises by 5 a year, every year. This means that A_1 will be 74, A_2 78, A_3 82 and so on – steady, persistent and appreciable church growth. If you could make r 0.3 then attendance would rise by 10 a year: 70-80-90 and so on. If r were 0.5 then revival would seem to have broken out!

So the way the numbers play out is that the biggest growth potential lies in working on the retention rate of those who try us out. Church growth is primarily about welcoming aboard those whom God is giving us to sail with us.

After five years the church that had a mission in Year 1 would have seen its attendance fall from 70 to 66; the church that succeeded in reversing the frequency decline would have stayed at 70; the church that stopped people leaving unless they died or left the area would be up to 75; the church that worked on increasing the throughput of visitors would still have an attendance of 70 (though fewer members and presumably less giving); but the church that worked on its retention rate would be up to an attendance of 90, and still growing.

That's why this course is primarily about the retention rate – how to welcome and integrate the already contacted or interested or attracted into the community of the church. But it also touches on each of the other factors involved in the growth of the church as we should not neglect any dimension, and they are all interlinked any way. Who knows, for example, how many people we see as visitors who may privately be thinking like those who are trying us out? And if we can improve the retention rate then evangelistic missions become much more effective, for those who make a faith-response are more likely to make it stick. And if we can help more people discover the church in the first place as well as increasing the retention rate then there will be even more growth.

In putting numbers into the simple algebraic equations I have attempted to describe the 'average' church. But there is no such thing in practice. Every church is unique. So you could if you wished work out the values for each factor in your own church and then work through the sums to uncover the dynamics where you are and so respond to them. Some factors are easy to find out – most churches record weekly attendance in their service registers and it is straightforward enough to average them over a period of time to give A. Membership (M) has to be gauged by taking an annual or bi-annual eight-week register of all people attending. People who know the congregation well will need to identify how many visitors there are each week and at peak times like Christmas and 'Back to Church Sunday'. You can discover frequency (f) from the average number of weeks your members attend during the eight weeks. Or else, if you know M, V and A you can calculate f from them. The vicar or minister and wardens or church council or pastoral team will need to get their heads together to work out who has left and who has joined in the last year (J and L). The hardest job is to estimate T and to distinguish T people from 'V' for visitors. It may be best to monitor this week by week.

Our web site gives some practical advice about how to go about such an exercise. But for the moment, I think we have shown how it is that the most important and promising way of growing the average church is the welcoming of strangers and newcomers. This, in turn, is simply a practical exercise in Christian love. Are we prepared to love our new neighbour or not?

Acknowledgements

Our grateful thanks to all those in Lichfield Diocese who were subjected to our early attempts with these materials in our Larger and Midi church conferences. Thanks also to those individual churches who allowed us to try out the materials – our hope is that as a result you have become more welcoming. This early trialling process sparked a multitude of conversations which informed our understanding of this area and helped to shape the course. We are also grateful to other missioners and church leaders who have provoked thought by their words and materials. Special thanks to Joan and Christine, our wives, who have supported and encouraged us in the gestation of this course.

Our thanks to Chris Loughlin who filmed and produced the DVD, and those who were filmed in this production, also to Christine Jackson who supplied the photos. We are also grateful to all those at Church House Publishing who have aided the production of this Training Course and especially to our ever helpful and professional editor Kathryn Pritchard.

Our hope and prayer is that through this course churches will be encouraged and equipped to welcome those who try them out and that in the family of the church they will find the welcoming heart of God.